Not Good Yet

Lessons From The First Six Months and One Hundred Comedy Performances of a Denver Open Mic Comedian

Mark Masters

Copyright © 2019
ISBN 978-0-9903947-1-6

DEDICATION

To my parents, none of this would be possible without you. Strong hugs!

Special thanks to open mic organizers everywhere, the comedians and audience members who attend open mics, and the wait staff at open mics, who have it worst of all.

TABLE OF CONTENTS

Not Good Yet, The Opener	1
What's In A Name	7
The Comedy Marathon Analogy	13
My First Open Mic	17
Your First Open Mic	25
The Open Mic Experience	37
New Talent Night in Denver	49
My Denver Comedy Class	59
My Denver Comedy Elders	65
The Transplant	67
The Elder Statesman	77
The Comedy Club Owner	85
Comedy Podcasts and Books	95
One Way To Gain Hosting Experience	105
Not on Facebook	111
Comedy Festival Visit	115
Comedy-Mecca Visit - New York City	127
Comedy-Mecca Visit - Los Angeles	143
Young Comics Steal Jokes	147
My Shows And Gigs As A Performer	165
Can You Learn Comedy?	171
Christmas Letter	177

The Big Show: Holiday Ha Ha Ha	181
Not Good Yet, The Closer	189
Thank You, Stay Connected	193
Appendix: Photos	195

Not Good Yet, The Opener

In the moment I find it annoying, the intrusion, my arms full and mind elsewhere, but the comment snaps me back into the present, and later I will cry, tears of gratitude, for what the stranger shared with me.

My name is Mark Masters, kind of, and this is a book I have wanted to write forever. When I was in elementary school an author visited our class. I still remember his book, a kids' fiction story. It was about a shed in the backyard where time almost stood still. An hour in the shed was like a second in the outside world.

The brothers who discovered this shed used it to their advantage to procrastinate on homework and other hijinks. I have thought about that shed at least a few times a year, for thirty plus years.

I have always wanted a shed like that. To be able to put the real world on pause and learn a new skill, a language, a bizarre but tedious parlor trick. Although I have never found one, I also never forgot about it. And recently, I found a loophole.

What if I just checked out from my real life, and spent six months as engrossed as possible in a weird, and wonderful world of my choosing? If I chose something inexpensive, I wouldn't even need that big a piggy bank.

The world I chose, comedy, already has gads of folks who engage it on love alone, with sub-poverty-level bank accounts. Library books, dive bar waters, and online video, it turns out, are all free.

Even better, if I kept it mostly secret from people in my "real" life, I could even pull off the neatest thing about that shed story: suddenly having a new and entertaining skill with what seemed like no time invested, no tears shed, no hard work.

Imagine the relief anonymity can provide when pursuing something that could fail spectacularly. What would you try if there were no consequences, nobody watching, or judging you?

I was under the misapprehension that this new pursuit would be all fun and games, and occasional light work. I mean, most of this is binge-watching comedy on Netflix, right?

I would learn that the illusion of not working hard would be just that, an illusion. Like the duck that shows no struggle above water, my churning metaphorical legs would pump with concomitant energy to a wickedly difficult task. I would work harder than most people have ever worked at anything in their life. And even so, in the end, I would be no Jerry Seinfeld. Turns out six months is nothing in comedy years.

I once had a talent manager in New York City literally recoil in disgust, a physical body action that was one part sneer, one part turning around one hundred and eighty degrees when I informed him I had been doing this for less than a year. I guess after hanging out with me and Jim Gaffigan and inspecting my gray hairs he was expecting better.

The other disheartening thing I did not see coming, really hurts. The more I studied, the more I became self-aware of how bad I was. In the beginning, your hubris gives you false hope. There is a common phenomenon where what is once a prized child, your favorite joke, the funniest thing you have ever come up with, with time, can become something you are ashamed of. Time is a funny thing in comedy and generally a very cruel mistress.

Comedy is complicated in this way. The better you get, the more you dislike how good you are. In the beginning, you don't even have the context to know you are terrible. You know you can make someone laugh at a party, how hard could it be if you have the advantage of a microphone and the undivided attention of an entire room? I had some public speaking experience already, surely making a few people laugh in Denver would be easy.

My misplaced confidence would only serve to diminish my education in the funny. Turns out this is a punishingly hard craft to hone. And the instantaneous feedback of failure is brutal. Soul crushing, even. But I had set up a weird kind of experiment where I could fail and hardly anyone I cared about would know about it. I was free in a sense to fail fast, to not-good more quickly.

And then a funny thing happened. I started to care about the Denver comics I was struggling alongside. I don't want to get all band of brothers here, but Shakespeare knew what was up. I was invested in not failing in front of these random strangers that I was becoming friendly with.

Although there was no shed, I did hide. I went by a stage name. I hung out in places nobody I knew would ever go. Another funny thing happened, maybe more predictable. The comic's life became more fun than my "real" life. I dove deeper down the rabbit hole. I started traveling to learn more: Las Vegas, New York City, Los Angeles. Exploring comedy at shows, talking to comedians, reading as many books and articles, watching as many documentaries, and movies, as I could get my hands on, became my obsession. I volunteered at a comedy festival in Atlanta, GA just to get closer to the beast.

Everywhere I went, I would seek out new opportunities to learn -- in Santa Fe, New Mexico; Tempe, Arizona; and Newport, Rhode Island. If I had a speaking opportunity from that past life, a travel obligation like a wedding or a family reunion, you would find me at 1 a.m. in a seedy bar at an open mic, talking to comics. Or at a show, soaking in the talent of stronger comedians.

In this pursuit, I ran past Gary Gulman, hung out with Jim Gaffigan, and saw Louis C.K. perform for 12 people. All of those happened in New York City by the way. Denver is still a great comedy scene, but boy, New York is a mecca. I've been twice during this pursuit and I itch to get back.

So that's the gist of this story. I spent six months working on a new performance skill. I stood behind a microphone in front of strangers, an incredibly scary proposition for most people, more than one hundred times. I improved in fits and starts. Partly by being a good documentarian myself.

I kept a spreadsheet with notes of every performance, most of which I recorded and re-listened to recently. I kept notebooks where I wrote notes on over one thousand short sets from other open mic comedians. I've pored over them recently, too. It was great preparation for this book.

I am six months in and I love this. I write (hopefully) funny stuff every day now, and this train shows no signs of slowing down. I still go to open mics many times a week. The more I write, the more I am eager to perform and to try out new material.

I even enjoy bombing a little bit, which I think is a good sign. My reaction to a quiet room with faces buried in phones is slowly turning from mild depression to an occasional "piss-off I know this is funny" attitude.

The only thing I still dislike is waiting and going up late. I wouldn't mind watching three hours of other comedians if I could go up at like 4 p.m. And yes, I realize I sound old. But I can tell in recordings how tired I sound after 1 a.m. I'm not at my best. And I'm not ready to abandon enough of my non-comedy life to sleep until noon.

I wanted to capture this moment, six months in, for posterity. The funny, wild, silly and maybe courageous stories that follow don't do it justice, but still, I hope they give you some idea of what I went through to get to where I am now, a truly mediocre comic. I promise you they are all true, even when I wish they were not.

In this book I'll relate lessons that will help those that might follow in my footsteps. A lot of them will be specific to my comedy hometown of Denver, but some are universal. I hope you will learn from my numerous mistakes and failures. You can start by not thinking that comedy will be easy. It is hard!

Writing a book is hard, too. But if this encourages even one person to find their own "shed" and pursue something with the undeniable love and passion I found for comedy in 2018, it will be worth it.

Along the way, I hope you laugh out loud, but I would also accept you quietly picking up your phone and reading something on it instead.

I'm used to that by now.

- Mark (December 25, 2018)

What's In A Name

This is a story about my stage name that I wrote for a collection of comedy short stories. I have since met Sam Tallent many times and seen him headline Comedy Works. He is a tour de force of comedy and a surprisingly sweet and wonderfully nice man.

Mark Masters is my stage name.

It isn't real. My actual name is ... well, that's none of your business.

I think most audiences realize Mark Masters is a stage name. Unless they think my parents were hoping for an adult entertainment star. Or a magician.

Some say the name is hacky. I like to think of it as memorable. An alliteration. Like that last sentence.

On stage, my stage name and I have been through a lot together. Offstage, we have our own identity and history. Which is surprising for a name I only asked to be memorable.

We'll get back to that, but let's start in the beginning. 2018 was my first year of stand-up. It was a lot of fun, but awful, too.

You meet a lot of great people. But you fail. Over and over. In public. For me and my stage name, that was mostly in noisy dive bars around Denver.

I spent a lot of time waiting in these places. Hours sometimes, for just a few minutes of mic time. And the hardest waits were the late ones.

One good thing about waiting when your material is weak is there is almost no one left to hear you. A host. A disinterested bartender. If you are lucky, one or two other sad souls. One bad thing about waiting when you crave stage time and experience is there is almost no one left to hear you.

I did a lot of waiting in one venue in particular. Lion's Lair on Colfax Avenue. The longest-running comedy open mic in Denver. It is one of the hardest, because the vibe can be ... unfriendly. I remember the first time I ever went. A host suggested another comedian should quit. Over the microphone. For all to hear.

The disinterest from other comedians can be acute. Most nights the comedians get as far from the stage as possible. Probably if they could hide under the pinball machine (The Shadow, 1994) they would.

For me, the most difficult aspect is the late start, 11 p.m. Once I had a 6 a.m. flight the next day. I badly wanted to go on stage early. But I didn't. The hosts at this mic pick names off the list however they like. I went up after all the names that were better known than mine. Few of which stuck around to see me struggle.

One time at Lion's Lair though, magic struck. I was called up early.

It was admittedly a feat of luck, no skill required. But when I got that chance, you better believe I took everything I had learned in more than fifty open mic experiences, to make the most of it.

Those experiences were at Denver bars like the White Whale, Irish Rover, El Chorito, 3 Kings, Syntax Physic Opera, and Black Buzzard. Great places if you compare them to the bars I arrived at to find the mic delayed, canceled, or more often than I care to admit, the venue permanently closed.

I can't overexpress my gratitude for the hosts of these mics who wait more than anyone else. They have to listen to every comic no matter how bad. They are the enablers of comedic exploration, and sometimes, but rarely, some of it is good.

My formative open mic experiences impacted what I did at Lion's Lair that night. But why was I called up so early? My first clue was revealed on the road.

I traveled to Atlanta to volunteer at, and attend, the Red Clay Comedy Festival. Some Denver comics were performing. Nathan Lund, Allison Rose, Geoff Tice, and Jeff Koehn. I would end up making a gift bag for Janeane

Garofalo among other duties. But first I had to find someone to tell me what to do.

My volunteer coordinator was running late on day one and tried to contact me on Facebook, a communication hub for almost every comedian.

But not me. Even today I've never been on it. Real name. Stage name. Any name. Never.

But in a classic Who's On First situation, she found another Denver based comedian named Mark Masters. He promptly Facebook messaged her back and confusion ensued. Once it cleared, he informed her that he had heard of this other Mark Masters.

And he made sure to tell her that he was in Denver at home for a reason. The newer Mark Masters, so he had heard, was funnier.

I couldn't believe it. Not only was there another Denver comic named Mark Masters, but there must also be a third one as well!

The festival was incredible, and I had a great time. I learned a ton from other comics. Once back in Denver I continued my first-year slog. Writing. Performing. Failing. Getting back up again. Wash. Rinse. Repeat.

I thought I had heard the end of other Denver comics named Mark Masters. But I was wrong. My stage name had one more trick for me.

It was a chilly fall night just after Halloween, and I was at Lion's Lair. My late arrival didn't discourage me from scrawling Mark Masters at the end of the list. As I found a stool at the bar, I noticed a buzz amongst the comics.
And not because it was the time T.J. Miller dropped in.

This time touring comic and local legend Sam Tallent was on hand, to co-host with Byron Graham. Early on Byron disappeared into the back room. Sam was left solo. He looked at the list to call up another comic and said:

"It's been awhile since I've seen this guy, let's welcome Mark Masters to the stage."

He was not talking about me. We had never met. But was I going to let that confusion stop me? No way! I rushed to the stage.

The place was packed, even up front, nobody had left yet. I stared out at the crowd, microphone in hand. Sam looked at me, quizzically. I stared into the distance, a bit overwhelmed.

A moment of quiet ensued.

I finally broke the silence. Progressed through my jokes. Told my stories sharpened by hours of stage time.
Earned a few minutes at a time, over many months, in numerous venues. Slung some new stuff too.

What's In A Name

I wouldn't say I crushed the room. But, I got some compliments after and earned a couple of good laughs from the back wall comics, many of whom had never stuck around to see me before.

Even better, I felt great the next day. Refreshed by a decent night's sleep.

2018 was the year I told my very first joke on any stage. I performed at Comedy Works downtown ahead of Josh Blue. Did stage time in six states. I even did a showcase set in New York City.

But the highlight may have been that night at Lion's Lair. Getting on stage early and meeting Sam Tallent.

All because of a name.

Mark Masters.

The Comedy Marathon Analogy

One reason I got into comedy was because of what I call the marathon analogy.

One of the most important events in my life was completing my first marathon. It is hack to make fun of casual endurance athletes, but I will defend to the death the life-changing implications of completing the impossible, when it is truly, the impossible. Not like the modern-day usage of literally, which no longer means what it should.

Imagine a nightmare scenario where you are at a high school track. In a sniper's nest above you is an expert marksman, with orders to kill you if you stop running, once you start. Your orders are to run 26.2 miles of laps or die trying.

Sure, some in shape people could make it over ten miles, but almost everyone would eventually physically or mentally break down and curl into a ball on the track. It would be literally impossible to complete the 26.2 miles for you, without specialized training.

Bang.

So there we have an impossible task. Can we transform our body into a machine that is capable of accomplishing this impossible task? And how would it feel to do so?

The Comedy Marathon Analogy

I can tell you from experience that almost anybody can transform their body in as little as a few months to accomplish this impossible. And it feels amazing to accomplish the impossible.

There comes a time in many adults' lives where life turns into a repeating series of the same things. There are no more grand accomplishments. As a kid, there are stages and checkpoints nearly every day, but as an adult, none of that. What a bore!

I once had a nickname in a ski town, "challenger", which was a good nickname. I like to think it really got to the heart of me. I love a challenge.

And comedy is a challenge like running a marathon, but in spades, or to stay in theme, on steroids. Thus my likening of comedy to running a marathon.

You can beat the marathon in as little as a few months of training. In comedy my six months of experience is a joke. It can take years and years to build up writing and performance muscles. There are checkpoint accomplishments on the way, like earning your first laugh, your first real comedy-club performance, and others. But the comedy treadmill never stops.

For a challenge junkie, this seems to be the hardest thing I could attempt. I would like to one day have two hundred people pay money to have me make them laugh. That is laughably absurd to the point of impossible to even imagine, right now.

Which is why I am on this journey.

To try and make the impossible possible.

The Comedy Marathon Analogy

My First Open Mic

Every aspiring comedian needs to start somewhere, and it is usually at an open mic. A free for all of learning and comedic exploration, often held in a business halfway to going out of business. A struggling open mic venue is the perfect metaphor for the misfits and malcontents that are often too optimistic about their futures as working comedians.

Sometimes your first time at an open mic goes unexpectedly well. But this is not always the case, and usually only delays the inevitable.

Many intrepid souls are ripe with hope as they approach the stage. But like an eager lamb to the slaughter, they are soon to be smacked in the face with a harsh reality. That when the rubber hits the road, when they are the performer behind the mic, this is not a Netflix special, this is not what they visualized, and instead of applause, they are greeted with the deafening silence of disinterested patrons.

They, and everyone within earshot, know for sure that they are not good. That was my experience my first time, and many times after, but my first time was especially not good.

The Irish Rover. June 25, 2018.

My First Open Mic

I get the light one minute earlier than I expect and now my time is up. I'm arguing with the host in front of all the other comedians. I finally relinquish the microphone, humiliated.

I went in with some confidence, optimistic for a much better outcome. But I was not good. Maybe because I was cut off before my big finish?

I thought that at the time, but with more experience, I realize now it wasn't that at all. Not enough laughs, too many words, premises too obscure, and more. The 'wrong list' is long. How did this happen?

Let's flashback.

New Year's Day, 2018. A forty-two-year-old writes down a bunch of crazy New Year's Resolutions.

Read fifty books, grow hair on my head, perform stand-up comedy in three states, and a few others.

In June I start to work on the stand-up. I read a book about joke writing. I read a book about stand-up comedy. I can hear all the comics groaning. Books are dumb. Learn on the mean streets, man.

Do you want to really groan? I start planning business cards. I haven't even done a single mic. I wouldn't learn until an episode of Crashing, four months later, that business cards in comedy are anathema. But they are what I am used to, and they do later help me book a paid gig. And just the idea imbues me with false confidence, so quit your judging.

Stand-up requires confidence when every data point you have tells you not to be confident. It turns out to be the ultimate fake it till you make it pursuit. I think. I'm still faking it, so check back another time to see if I ever make it.

My set is a three-page typed document. I use Google Docs. I have three bits. Callbacks. Popular culture references so fresh they include Angela Lansbury. I'll wait while ninety percent of you google who that is. DNA tests, Red Lobster, and Airbnb are my topics.

I practice in front of a mirror. While I drive. In my head at the grocery store.

I go to my first open mic to see what this stuff is all about. There is a website that tries to list them all for Denver and surrounding areas (5280comedy.com). I don't know it at the time but I am lucky the mic is actually happening. At times twenty-five percent of the information on the website is wrong.

3 Kings Tavern is a rock and roll venue in the South Broadway section of Denver. There is often a dog or two roaming around what a tour guide might generously call authentic patrons. Kitty corner from the band stage is a small three-foot by three-foot stage in a corner by the sidewalk. It faces a row of disinterested bar sitters, a few pool tables, and a booth holding some comedians.

My First Open Mic

Tonight I talk to a bar patron, who just moved from Miami, and we play some pool. Nearly everyone these days in Denver just moved from somewhere. When I'm asked if I would ever get up on stage, with an actual pit in my stomach, I say yes, I'm planning to. It is hard to remember now how nervous I was, almost physically sick.

The comedians that night are so-so. A couple are downright terrible, but they are leagues ahead of me, getting up behind the mic. The bad ones embolden me though, I can do better than they did, right?

That was a Friday night, the Monday following I am a few doors down at the Irish Rover to watch again. Here there isn't even a stage, just a cleared area of the dining room floor and a microphone. Somehow this environment seems better suited to comedy though. Perhaps because the space is smaller.

Orin Be, a Philadelphia transplant who on other nights bartends at the Rover, is the host. He runs through comedians giving them four minutes each.

I sit as close as I can to the action and get singled out frequently. I later learn that almost everyone in the bar is a comedian I would soon know by name. Being the only "civilian" who has never heard the mostly regurgitated jokes makes me a popular target. Some comedians lock in on me, and only me, while they work on their recycled material.

When I go to feed the meter in my car you can sense some disappointment in the crowd, and when I return an uptick from mild depression to slightly warmer mild depression.

I specifically remember Uncle Paulie using me in a series of jokes about a penny. Andy Hamilton locks in on me and gets some legitimate laughs from me.

In one week I would get up on this stage. I studied how the timing works, how the list appears to work, how the mic stand works. I take some notes. I am scared, but I see enough bad stuff that I have an attitude that at least I shouldn't be the worst.

I arrive early on Monday, June 25 and put my name on the list, I am the tenth name, but I will be called thirty-first. I wait three and a half hours to get my four minutes.

I get a nice welcome when I announce this is my first time ever, and a generous laugh at my first joke and then it is disinterest as I plod through what I would now consider very slow material. I can't believe no one cracks up at my Angela Lansbury reference. Remember her?

I get the light, a waving cell phone, at two and a half minutes. I was expecting it a minute later. I must have missed an announcement at some point that the last folks won't get as much time as everyone else. I would later learn, and even respect, that folks as bad as me, can get rushed for the benefit of everyone else. At the moment it really throws me for a loop. I don't know what to do.

Even six months later I often struggle to adjust material on the fly. A stronger comedian might be able to, but my material is pretty heavily scripted and timed out. With a few minutes before getting on stage I can usually rewrite my setlist, but under the lights, behind the microphone, I am not comfortable enough yet to think about anything but delivering my prepared jokes.

There is a funny thing I wasn't aware of before I started all of this. Microphone amnesia? Not sure what people call it or if it has a real name. But basically when you get off the stage, in the beginning, you can't remember anything, it is exactly like blacking out from drinking. Recording yourself can be your only proof that you were on stage.

It takes about a month before I can even remember a single audience reaction from memory. Months later I can actually watch different faces as I deliver material, and even adjust pacing, the hardness of punchlines, and more, in real time. It is a significant improvement. But for now, I suck at just about everything.

3 minutes in and this is quickly turning into a steaming pile of humiliation. It gets worse when I get the second and more aggressive light. Over six months I hope that Orin has forgotten the small tantrum I threw. We have since performed together in Breckenridge and he has been generous with tips and advice.

I get off stage and another comic is up. This is a fast food restaurant at this point. Get 'em up, move 'em out. I'm so disappointed in myself. I consider quitting.

But not before I review the recording and my notes.

I took notes on every comedian before me. Mostly on paper, but some in just my head. Thoughts about how the better ones were able to command attention, earn some laughs. I use a large yellow covered notebook, like a grade-schooler might carry to school. I eventually will fill it with pages of joke ideas, open mic notes, and more. The first notebook covers notes up until August 13, 2018.

Something neat happens after that first performance. Watching comedians after it, I can make more impactful observations. Something about the experience of having done comedy, makes my viewing of comedy, with a lens on my own improvement, so much more meaningful.

I recorded that first set. I listen to it on my shameful drive home. The opening laughs, like a golfer making a good putt on a terrible day, are what will bring me back. The next week, guess where I will be? At the Irish Rover.

I'm not quitting yet. I still think I can do this. The band-aid has been ripped off, and away we go.

And one thing is definitely for sure.

I am not good yet.

Your First Open Mic

Things in life worth doing are difficult, and that includes doing your first open mic. In this chapter, I will take you through my first open mic focusing on what you can expect and how you can make your dream of open mic comedy come true.

The first time I attended a comedy open mic was a Friday night early mic at 3 Kings, which you might remember is a rock and roll dive bar in the South Broadway area of Denver. The kind of bar where dogs roam around pinball machines, and they have a bouncer at the door pretty much at all times.

Watching the other comedians makes my stomach hurt.

Just watching other comedians do open mic comedy is physically painful to me.

If they do well, I think I could never do that. If they do poorly I feel so badly for the poor bastard on stage, it hurts me inside.

But something about the really bad folks is encouraging. They might be terrible for two minutes and then say something that makes me laugh out loud. The inconsistency makes me feel like I could maybe do this.

It would be a while before I realized what I saw that night was a comedian working out new material sandwiched around a solid A joke that had been told many times before. With hindsight goggles, the signs are clear. But as one of the only "civilians" (somebody not going on stage), I was clueless.

Now I can observe the audience, and if I see other comics not laughing, or maybe giving a chortle that sounds more dismissive than appreciative, I can surmise that the material is well worn.

But at the time, the less polished performances embolden me to try myself, which I do a week or so later at the Irish Rover.

What can you learn from my experience? Let's cover some of the basics.

Many mics have a few key players, the most important is the host, who has a list. This will include many names. Always introduce yourself to a host that doesn't know you or possibly doesn't remember you. If in doubt, introduce yourself again. Let them know it is your first time (if it is) and that you have some basic questions. How much time do you get? How will you know when to go up? Should you re-introduce yourself later in the night? How does the light work?

As a first-timer, you will probably go up pretty late, and I found this impossibly difficult in the beginning. It wasn't only the wait, it was also the listening to all the comedians before me. All that comedy content scrambled my brain to the point where I couldn't remember material that I had down cold before entering the bar.

With this in mind, know you probably need to know your material twice as well as you think, because of the comedy overload that will short circuit your brain while waiting.

Another approach to combat this would be to find a very small mic for your first mic. I didn't do this, but maybe I should have. The downside to this is probably a smaller audience, but it doesn't really matter. That's the most important thing I can say. The important thing is to get up. And resolve to do it again. In the beginning, anything else won't matter, even though paradoxically, at the moment, it seems like the most important thing in the world.

Bringing friends is an interesting topic. You might like to have some support, but it may turn into a crutch. Eventually, you will be performing without friends in the audience, so why not rip off the band-aid now? You probably don't want your friends seeing your first performance anyways if you can avoid it.

At a mic, you may want to network with other comedians ("hang") which is easier if you are solo, but you shouldn't really focus on this for the first few mics unless you can find someone you know is also in their first few mics.

Your First Open Mic

You should be paying attention to the performances, watching like an eagle.

Finally, on friends, and I apologize for revealing this secret, but if the host knows you have a lot of friends in the audience, they will (correctly so) make you go up last, or within a few spots of last. That might have happened anyways, but your friends turn out to be a sacrificial gift you are giving the community, more established comedians need them to practice material on.

I guess what I am saying is that selfishly, I hope you bring fifty friends, but your very first time, consider going solo.

Lists run in different ways. The most straight-forward but most rare is one that is first come first served. The White Whale in Denver (hosted by Alan Bromwell) often runs this way.

Usually, the host (also known as an MC, short for the master of ceremony), will do some material at the outset, then introduce comedians.

Sometimes between acts, especially after very bad ones, the host may tell some more jokes to "reset the energy" of the room. My favorite hosts are fast between comedians, but also funny, they tell a one-liner that feeds off the material or the person that just was on stage. The worst hosts talk too much between comedians without adding any value.

I have been to an out-of-town mic that exclusively used a "God mic" to move the show along. That is where the host talks into the mic from off stage. It is less personal but it is expeditious.

There are mics that run in random order, as chosen by the host, and you have to be ready to go up at any time. This can be fun in a chaotic way, but I find it difficult. It makes video recording almost impossible. On the other hand, I believe the old adage is true and it makes you a stronger comedian (as long as it does not kill you).

I much prefer the more common "up in two" scenario where a host will come over and tell you, that you are up in two. Let's look at an example:

> Jack (currently performing)
> Jill (up next)
> You (up in two)

When you are up next (like Jill, above) it is common to approach the stage, maybe position yourself off to the side and be ready to go on.

Sometimes you might get an extra-early indicator like up in five. Sometimes the host will read the upcoming comics in batches of five. There are lots of variations and soon you will be ready to handle any system. Knowing the most common ones increases the chances of you not being surprised or missing your spot.

When it is time to go on stage, shake the hand of the host. This takes some planning. Are both your hands full? Plan ahead. I like to leave my recording devices in the audience. Maybe when this book comes out my phone will finally be stolen, but so far so good, and I find it better captures audience reaction and how you sound out in the crowd.

If you take the mic out of the mic stand be sure to get it back in before you are done and welcome the host back to the stage. I still make this mistake because I get caught up in my act. Ideally, I would always have a short closing joke and would put the mic in as I started it.

If you are early to a mic, it is a great idea to go practice with the mic stand. They are all different. Be sure you know how to adjust the height and you can remove and put the mic back into it. Sometimes very experienced hosts will adjust the stand height for you as you approach, but this is rare.

Sometimes a mic stand is broken and can not be adjusted. You can learn this by testing it, or by observing other comedians. Your backup plan, in this case, is to remove the microphone from the stand and to move it somewhere behind you. Do not leave the mic stand in front of you without a mic in it.

Shake the hand of the host as you get off the stage. Whether you verbally thank the host or the comics before you at the start or end of your set is personal preference. I would say don't do it. And definitely, don't ask the audience to "give it up" for anything at the start of your set. Just do your material. Stage time is precious, respect and use it fully to understand what is working in your material and what is not.

If you are at a three-minute mic and you finish your material in two minutes, just finish. Don't be that person that ooh's and ahh's about how they don't have any more material. Giving back time to the community can earn you applause, try it sometime. Respect the time of everyone else. It should go without saying not to go over time either.

Definitely ask how much time you will have before you go up. I like to run a timer during other comedians sets before I go up, which accomplishes a few things. The straight forward is that it tells me how the mic is run so I can predict my experience when I go up. Sometimes a three-minute spot with a light at two minutes, is run like a German train system, and other times it is pretty haphazard. Sometimes there is talk of a light but it is never given despite your time running out. So watching how things are run lets me know what to expect for myself.

A more nuanced benefit of this is as an audience member. Sometimes I can't believe a comedian is still on stage and when I look they are only halfway done, so I make note of what I am not enjoying about their stage performance. On the other hand, sometimes I lose track of time during a performance and am shocked that several minutes have gone by. Try to be the latter when you get up.

The "light" is usually a phone flashlight or just the face of a phone. Depending on how bright the stage lights are, if you are lucky enough to perform on a legit stage (or unlucky), you may not be able to see it. Watch the host in acts before you, when the host gives the light see if the comedian acknowledges the light. That can tell you if it is visible from the stage.

Sometimes you will just see their reaction as body language, other people physically or verbally acknowledge the light to let the host know they understand. You can see this behavior at professional comedy clubs too if you watch closely. Sometimes it is a single finger that points from the mic, a head nod, or the most subtle: just redirecting your gaze towards the source of the light.

Stage lights (different from the light a host gives you) are an interesting problem for beginning comedians. I found them to be terrifying when I was starting out. OK, they are still terrifying! Know that if you walk closer to the front of the stage and if you shield your eyes you can usually see past them into the audience.

Telling jokes and not hearing any response, and not being able to see your audience, can be a blessing or a curse. I'd prefer to see my audience, it helps me modulate energy or even perhaps change my set list on the fly to try and attract attention, but that's advice for way past your first mic.

The odds are pretty good that you will "blackout" during your first time on stage. You will remember very little of it. That is why we are lucky that recording devices are so ubiquitous. Always make an audio recording of every set and listen to it. Dissect it. Look for the positive and the negative.

If you can video record sets, that's great, also do a similar analysis. I have a small GoPro with a small portable tripod (less than six inches tall) that I often set up. One of my favorite things about the video is that I can see audience reactions too, depending on where the camera is placed. I study them as much as I study myself on stage. Many comedians use their phone to record video, sometimes just propping the phone against a glass or other object.

The "blackout" will eventually go away but it can come back, like the first time you perform at a comedy club perhaps. Do make sure you know your material backward and forward so nerves do not derail you. You don't have to do this forever but there is no shame in bringing a typed out script as a security blanket and reading from it on your very first performance. Don't make it a habit though.

Be nice to everyone you meet. Always. The DJ, the host, other comedians, other audience members, wait staff, bartenders, everyone. In six months if you are lucky they will be running mics and shows and hosting podcasts, and you will be glad you were nice. Odds are very good that you are not funny enough yet to have an attitude.

Here is an out-of-the-box suggestion I did and loved. Once you realize you are sticking with this pursuit, go buy a microphone, a mic stand, and a cable. You can get all of that for under a hundred dollars, and if you buy used, for much less than that.

I think of this like the high school football running back with fumble problems that has to carry a football all day at school. Whenever you can, hold the mic, practice getting it in and out of the stand. Get comfortable with your new friend. Practice your routines from start to finish with the mic, stand, and cable. You don't want to learn on stage for the first time that an act out leaves you tangled up in the mic cable. For me, this little hack has helped me be a lot more comfortable on stage.

This is just one example of an overall piece of advice. Practice way more than you think you should. Mic time is incredibly precious with a real audience. Put in the work before you get there to make the most of it. You want to look like you are making things up on the fly, but paradoxically that can often come from more serious preparation.

The closing bit of advice I have for you is to start out your first ever set by saying this is your very first open mic ever. You only get one chance to do this and you will likely be greeted with tremendous positive energy. The folks in the room have all been there and they know what you are going through.

Tonight they will be nice to you. But next time, you better be funny!

I'm so excited for you and encourage you to send me a story of your first time going up.

Your First Open Mic

The Open Mic Experience

If you want to see a good slice of America, go to an open mic comedy night. Arrange for a designated driver though, you'll probably want to drink to make it through to the end. I have been to about a hundred open mics and I have seen some stuff, and met some people, that I won't soon forget.

I love the open mic scene. These are my people. Weirdo's, outcasts, and rebels. Silly, smart ... surprisingly smart, people. Talented, dedicated people. And drunks, and the almost homeless, and the wealthy bucket listers (that phrase confused me for a while, it means someone crossing off an item on their bucket list), people who lost bets, and people trying out a New Year's Resolution.

Let's get back to smart. I recall riffing with a comedian about Mark Twain and making a Roger "Clemens" quip. He didn't miss a beat. These men and women are overwhelmingly intelligent. If you want a great book or movie recommendation ask an open mic'er. They have great taste.

Sometimes they aren't even men or women, and I don't mean because of the modern thinking on gender. We have a sixteen-year-old teenager in our scene, she's very funny and poised. I saw a thirteen-year-old young man do a bit about masturbation in Los Angeles.

Like I said, I've seen some things. Let's run through some of them.

Face/Off

Like the time someone took their face off. I was at Syntax Physic Opera in Denver and a pretty good comedian who looked like he had been in a fire went up. He had something going on with his face, but it wasn't obvious what, and I didn't care. He told funny jokes. He told stories about having a lot of surgeries. Then as a punch line he literally pulled his face off, it was a prosthetic. You could see into his nose and eye cavity like he was a skeleton. The bit was about scaring kids at Halloween and I howled with laughter.

One man's dream ...

I remember another time at Syntax Physic Opera which usually has about forty people in attendance when it starts, almost all comedians, and dwindles to under ten people by the time I usually get to go on stage. But one time there were over fifty people when I went up. Fifty people!

The comedian before me was offensive, and not very funny, and the crowd just went flat. The host came out and said "give it up for [name]" and nobody clapped. She said "I don't know what just happened but your next comedian is ..." and she brought me on stage to silence.

This was close to the largest audience I had ever performed for and I did great with well-practiced material. I have a video of it I am very proud of. When the host came back on stage there was loud applause for me. She said, perhaps with some surprise in her voice, "that was great!". It was a terrific feeling to perform in front of so many people and make them laugh.

Comedy is like golf in that the small victories make all the less-than-stellar times more than worth it. I later found out the reason that so many people were there. The comedian who went two people after me had finished in last place in his fantasy football league and this was his punishment. About forty-five people had come out to see him.

Interesting, that his worst nightmare and punishment, is my dream.

Worst night ever

Probably the worst open mic experience for a comedian is when you arrive at a venue that is closed. I always endeavor to get the best information from online, but it is not always accurate. Multiple times I have driven to an open mic venue listed online only to find it shuttered, not even open for normal business.

(We are lucky in Denver to have a central website, even if it is not perfect. Many scenes don't even have a central place for comedy open mic information. Meghan

DePonceau is the local comedian that runs the site, yay Meghan)

I've also gone to other businesses and found them open, but with no mic running. Once at Lost Highway Brewing, two of us showed up to a defunct mic and we put on a show without a microphone to two people at the bar (one was the bartender). I actually worked out a joke I still tell about pillows there, and got a great idea for it from the customer at the bar, in discussion afterward.

The worst story though took place in San Francisco. I took a Lyft from Sunnyvale to try and hit a mic that was listed online. I even emailed a contact through Eventbrite to confirm it, but when I got there the place was closed up with one of those roll down garage-like doors, common in neighborhoods where windows are covered with bars. I waited for two hours outside as I patiently observed drug deals conducted, homeless people relieve themselves and more. The venue never opened.

I finally bailed and went over to the Punchline thirty minutes early for their open mic like event. I waited there for several hours and never even figured out how to sign up.

From there I went to an Irish bar and got my name on a list, but a couple of hours later had to leave for a 1 a.m. flight out of SFO. I scratched my name off the list on my way out.

Three attempts, zero minutes stage time.

Not a great open mic night.

Not that way

I love traveling and experiencing the open mic culture in other cities. Without knowing anyone it can be harder to get into conversations about why jokes worked or didn't, or just enjoy the "hang" at an Open Mic. (If you want to see how pros do this with controversial material, check out a great web series where you can watch comedians workshop bits in a casual setting called Inside Jokes put together by Andrew Schulz, on YouTube).

Despite not knowing anyone, I have found it can be pretty easy to approach a stranger and explain you are from out of town and get into a good conversation. If you ever have an out of town stranger say hi to you, be nice, help them learn about your scene. Thank you to everyone who has done so for me, I will definitely pay it forward.

A weird thing to me about big-city open mics is having to pay for stage time and weird rules about when you can arrive and leave.

My weirdest comedy tourism open mic story happened in Los Angeles. It was a late mic, on a surprisingly cold fall night in the city of angels, with the temperature in the 40's. The club was Ha Ha Comedy Club in Hollywood.

The Open Mic Experience

I got there early and paid five dollars to get my name put in a bucket. There was about half an hour to kill and I had a nervous energy about performing in front of new people and was excited to imagine who might be in the audience at night in Los Angeles.

I poked my head in the showroom, and it was huge! This was a real legit club, not some coffee shop, actor's closet, or dive bar. I nervously asked if it was OK to video record my set. A lot of times at clubs there are strict rules about video recordings, and often the clubs sell you their own recordings (which would have been fine). I was thrilled when the host told me it was no problem at all, of course I could record.

Finally, the host announced to the crowd that it was time to start the mic.

I made an excited beeline for the showroom.

A loud call from the host interrupted me. He yelled that I should follow him. I figured we were going to chill in some green room. Fun. But nope.

Instead, I was led by the kitchen, out a back door, and into an alley on the side of the club where there was a makeshift outdoor stage. Once outside I had to sit in the nearly freezing cold without a coat for two hours while I waited for my opportunity to sling jokes to a frigid, rather disinterested audience.

As an amusing, additional kick to the teeth, about every fifth name pulled out of the bucket turned out to be an actor or actress who by my interpretation was just paying for some stage time and recognition.

One gentleman did some kind of avant-garde short one-man play on stage, another woman did a monologue and some singing. It was weird.

At least the host was funny at the outset, and I got to see a thirteen-year-old perform. At the end of the day, it was stage time, and I loved it, despite the difficult conditions.

To have an opportunity to make strangers laugh is a gift, no matter the conditions.

Music Mic

Another out-of-town experience cemented for me how much I enjoyed performing stand-up comedy. I am a square when it comes to drugs and alcohol, but I have heard many comedians with ample drug experience relate that making other people laugh is the best high in the world. There really isn't anything quite like it.

I was in Santa Fe, New Mexico where my friend Dan had just married his sweetheart Rebecca. It was Sunday night, and almost everyone from the wedding had scattered back to wherever it was they came from after a weekend of celebrating. I was tired, and hung over, and was just back from Meow Wolf and some other errands when it occurred to me I could try to find an open mic.

I hopped online and in just a few minutes I found a music open mic about a ten-minute drive away that ended in fifteen minutes. Again, I was tired, hung over, and yearning for a good night's rest before the next day's six-hour drive to Denver. It didn't take more than a few seconds to decide. I swung into action and was out the door and in my car within minutes. Nothing seems to motivate me like the prospect of stage time!

When I arrived at Tiny's Restaurant & Lounge there was a party going on. A six-or seven-piece band was backing up anyone who wanted to get on stage and do a kind of live Karaoke thing and sing to a floor full of dancing partners.

I put my name on a list and had a beer at the bar. During a break, I introduced myself to the band and explained I was a comedian from Denver and asked if I could do five minutes of jokes. They said definitely and that they had about thirty more minutes of music and then I could close the night out.

I sat those next thirty minutes at the bar incredibly nervous. My nerves have improved over time, but they are worse in unfamiliar situations.

I had no idea if these fifty-plus strangers wanted to hear comedy, would boo me off the stage, or what. I could see they were incredibly passionate about music and dancing.

When I was announced and got on stage I used the wrong microphone, and I didn't realize it until a few minutes in. It was a pencil or cigar style microphone and not a vocals microphone. At that time I wasn't comfortable enough on stage to figure out how to swap to a better one. What a disaster.

Every time I tried to raise my voice it sounded terrible so I had to try and low energy deliver some high energy material.

But the crowd was very nice, and ultimately I think they enjoyed my performance. I got scattered applause as I said good night to Santa Fe.

I don't know what that band was called, but if they ever read this, thank you for the stage time and the hospitality.

Stand-up surprise

Voodoo Lounge is an improv theater with a weekly open mic that was once run by Nicolai Roscoe who moved onto New York City and is now run by Ben Bryant. Both are incredibly talented hosts, who always have brilliant opening material and funny quips between performers.

I've seen some interesting stuff at this theater, maybe because the open mic is discoverable by more than open mic comedians, due to its improv business and downtown location.

Here I've watched performers who drove down from Wyoming, and a high-school student who I saw twice.

One night there was a ramp up to the stage and a reconfiguration of the theater seating to accommodate a performer who got on stage by wheelchair. I think he was probably the most memorable.

Because after he rolled up on stage, he unexpectedly leaped out of the wheelchair and took the mic.

It was a comedy miracle! Actually, it turned out that his Muscular Dystrophy made it difficult for him to stand for long periods of time. He was pretty funny.

A modest proposal

Sometimes there are remarkable performances. I have seen a comedian try and eat two cans of whipped cream during a three minute set at the Lion's Lair, while a gentleman with an outrageous multi-colored mohawk tried to help.

I have seen a comedian hawking wares like a used landline phone out of a backpack of treasure, at the Irish Rover, to the howling approval of the audience. The same comedian once gave a lecture to the audience at a pizza shop on a Saturday night about how you measure drugs, and all the nicknames and synonyms you need to know, it was like a street-smart TED talk.

Of course, I have seen bombs, first-timers who forget their material and panic on stage. I have seen people drop the mic by accident and on purpose (never do this, by the way). I have seen people so drunk they can barely stand, let alone get out an intelligible thought. I have seen nudity and folks in outrageous costumes, I have heard people talk in detail about their genitalia, and others talk about their children. I have even seen a Mog, half man half dog, do stand-up at an open mic.

Open mics are wildly entertaining in small doses, and in large doses, they are a grind, but a grind I wouldn't trade for anything in the world.

Probably the wildest thing I ever saw at an open mic was at Lion's Lair again, a comedian went on stage and launched into a not very punchy story about the last time he had been on the stage, years earlier.

Lion's Lair is the longest-running mic in Denver, it has been running continuously on Monday nights for over ten years.

The comedian on stage told a story about meeting a girl outside the bar and sharing a smoke and how they dated and how she stuck with him through some kind of hospitalization.

The Open Mic Experience

It was rambling and confusing but was about to get interesting.

He called her out in the crowd, dropped to one knee, and asked her to marry him.

Probably my favorite moment of the whole thing was the crowd reaction. You would expect cheering.

Didn't happen.

You would expect video recording. Happened in spades.

The audience, which was about 30 open mic comedians and a couple of randoms, for the most part, low-key booed and jeered. Man, what a cynical crew! Myself, I clapped sparingly.

The couple on stage was unaware of the room sentiment and hugged and cheered and left the bar. The next several comics made room in their sets for making fun of the couple.

I said Lion's Lair was the longest running open mic, not the friendliest.

New Talent Night in Denver

Your town may have something like New Talent Night at Comedy Works in Denver, Colorado. A real functioning comedy club that opens its doors for performers that may someday become something, or more likely will never make it out of the minor-league farm system.

Your town may have bringer shows to get you stage time at a real comedy club. Or you may travel to a nearby city that does.

Some cities like Colorado Springs hold a traditional Open Mic night at their club (Loonee's) where you can just show up, sign up, and get on stage. New Talent Night in Denver, is a whole other animal, as you will soon see.

Below I will explain how New Talent Night in Denver worked for me. It will be inside baseball that Denver comedians will appreciate and may have residual benefit for you, too. This could change in the future, but the foundation has a very long history.

I should start by explaining what Comedy Works is. The downtown club is legend. Set in Larimer Square in downtown Denver, Colorado, it has seen Joe Rogan, Dave Atell, and many other famous comedians record comedy albums there. Dave Chappelle performs there. Ali Wong. Aziz Ansari. It is small and intimate and in my eyes on par with The Cellar in New York City.

New Talent Night in Denver

There is a thought that the more of a fire hazard a comedy club is, the better it is for live comedy. Low ceilings, a dungeon-like setting, and tight seating all contribute to the psychology of a good comedy show. When the audience feels like they are somewhere special, where it is safe to let go and laugh, magic can happen. Great acoustics, phones protected in pouches, and alcohol, especially alcohol, all help create this environment.

And amazingly anyone can get up on stage at Comedy Works Downtown. All you have to do is call a phone number and leave your name. And again. And again. Usually, about eight weekly calls will do the trick, and then on that next call when the machine recording relays the lineup, you will hear your name on it. When it happened to me, I called back in to double check I had heard correctly. I was SO excited.

Your first time up you are a Newbie (N) and you get two minutes of time. The sound booth will light you at 2 minutes and your mic will be cut in the next 30 seconds or so depending on how you are doing and the mood of folks. I once saw Deacon Gray sprint to tell the sound booth to cut the mic of a woman who was performing, immediately. She had to complete her closing punchline without amplified audio.

Deacon Gray passed away in late 2018 but was the New Talent Night coordinator for over a decade, he was an institution. I have heard great things about him from many people.

Unfortunately, my first run in with Deacon was negative. He was dismissive and mean to me, like he was hazing a new fraternity member, perhaps. I had asked what I thought was a reasonable question about how to get the video of my performance (the answer: there is an email address you send a request to that leads to a payment process and receipt of video). While he was berating me for not reading the signage in the green room (I had, there was no mention of videos at the time, which he verified with some frustration), another comedian congratulated me on a good set, which made the whole interaction even more bizarre.

In his defense, and I did not know this at the time, he was very sick and would die within a few months. In light of this I feel lucky to have ever met him, and even more glad that despite our interaction, I gave him a Thank You card later because I knew that Comedy Works stage time would not have happened without him.

Unfortunately, the video run-in was not our only conflict on my first night up at Comedy Works.

When he was in charge, which he was for my first performance, there were notes given towards the end of the show. They happened once all the amateurs were done, while stronger performers started. Notes took the form of constructive criticism and advice about individual performances. I would later learn that they were often curt, and more criticism than constructive.

Unfortunately, nobody told me there were notes or to be at a certain place at a certain time and I missed it completely. What he scribbled down about me, is, for now, a mystery to me. I often think about trying to find that piece of paper with the help of Comedy Works.

But on this night, I sat, blissfully ignorant of "Notes" in the back row of the club watching the professionals, while others huddled in the green room, backstage with Deacon. Unnoticed by me, the list of performers backstage had a right-justified hint ("Notes") to the side of the left-justified performers, that looked like an instruction for the MC.

When Deacon and I passed in the hallway later, he let me know dismissively that "you missed notes", and I asked him what he meant. Suffice to say his explanation was not very kind. He had a clipboard in his hand with his notes, and when I told him I would very much like to get feedback from someone like him, he looked at his clipboard, and then me, and said: "I don't have time, I need to go."

I nearly cried. The nervous energy of being on stage that night and the dismissiveness of what I perceived to be a gatekeeper for Denver comedy was enough to really put a damper on what should have been a very special night for me.

Luckily, a number of my friends (twenty-six) had come out to see me and many of us went out for drinks after, and mostly the incident was forgotten.

I would later attend a special show in his honor, in the last days he was on this earth. Comedians who had been touched by his skill, and talent, and capacity to teach, came onto stage one after another and roasted him, told touching stories, and funny jokes.

Aside from a conversation I had with the owner of Comedy Works, Wende Curtis, after his death, where her appreciation of his impact on the community was obvious, it was probably the most important event that cemented his legacy in my mind.

I find it unfortunate I didn't get more time to overlap with him. From listening to him on podcasts I think I would have enjoyed--if given the time of day--to break down jokes with him, and to observe his analytical ability.

He created a system at Comedy Works like rungs in a ladder that persists to this day and is unlike anything I am aware of in the rest of the country.

The hierarchy of performers in the Comedy Works universe impacts your New Talent Night appearance cadence, and time on stage:

N - Newbie, two-minute sets
C - three-minute sets, eight-to-ten weeks apart

B - four-minute sets, (more regular appearances) six-to-eight weeks apart
A - Almost famous, five minutes (I think, don't quote me)
Headliner - ten-minute set

When you call in, the lineup is only announced for N, C, and B. Sometimes someone will be working on a late night tape and get a seven-minute set or a different amount of time, too, but that is only for A's and above. A's are assigned in a process you don't need to care about yet at your level. Also, I don't know it, so that works out for both of us.

The list will "drop" (be hung up) right before show time backstage, which is when you can see your order and who is headlining. If a performer doesn't check-in, in time, some lucky performer from the standby list will get on, and they will learn of this when the list is posted. Also, this is when the MC for the night finds out they are hosting.

Comedy Works does an incredible job making an entertaining show and gathering an audience. It is a gift to be able to perform on the Comedy Works stage, and often comedians with comedy albums, late-night TV credits, or other industry credits, are mixed in with first-timers.

Once you reach A level you can be invited to host shows, including for nationally touring comedians. Comedy Works has a South location also, in Greenwood Village, Colorado. That room is larger, is cavernous, and more suburban. It tends to have more TV-famous comedians and fewer comedy fan comedians. Occasionally New Talent Night can be at the South location. If you perform there be ready for a more conservative older crowd, generally.

Moving up the hierarchy is important if you want to be almost famous, and from what I have gathered, works as follows. All of this could change or I could have heard wrong.

Almost always after one Newbie performance, your next appearance will be at the C level. I guess if something is truly awful about your performance you might have to repeat your Newbie set, but in my first six months, I never saw that occur.

Moving from C to B is a decision by the New Talent Coordinator, so at the moment I am not sure if that is even happening. I believe that your performance in the annual New Faces competition, a several-month-long comedy competition drives this as well.

Moving from B to A is a promotion made by Comedy Works Staff.

I treat my New Talent Nights as an opportunity to bring friends out to watch me, and it is a fun, regular milestone to track my improvement. You can do similar in your town.

New Talent Night in Denver

Even if you do not have a fancy comedy club like we are lucky enough to have in Denver, you probably have local showcases which are organized by showrunners. My only advice there is don't ask to be put on a show. When it is your time you will be recognized and you will be grateful that you didn't go up earlier.

In my first six months, I have never asked to be put on a show and I don't plan to ever ask in my local scene until I am booked on one. Sounds like a catch-22, but someone will notice me when I'm ready for it, I have faith. In the meantime, as you will read later, I started organizing my own shows. Workaround!

One thing that is more fun at the tail end of my six months is that when I call in about New Talent Night, I recognize more and more names on the lineup lists. This is a product of going to so many open mics and becoming a member of my local comedy community. It is especially fun to hear someone in my own comedy class announced for their newbie set. Sometimes I even recognize promotions from C to B, which is very exciting.

There is a standby list for every show and part of the "comedy culture" is to put your name on the list and see and be seen backstage before the show. It is a festive environment and although the odds are very low of being pulled off the standby list onto the lineup, it is a lot of fun to hang around.

Once the show starts there is great instructional value in watching all the performances from newbies, up to, if you are lucky, a winner of Last Comic Standing (Josh Blue on my night) or best-selling author and television star (Adam Cayton-Holland).

Occasionally there are other opportunities for amateur stage time at Comedy Works. Thick Skin is a weekly show currently hosted by Mike Stanley (previously Greg Baumhauer) and a rotating group of friends. It includes an amateur bucket opportunity for four minutes of stage time. I definitely encourage you to find any opportunity to stretch your legs past the open mic scene and find stage time in front of paying audiences. It is a different kind of experience.

The last thing I will mention about New Talent Night is "Clean December". In the month of December because of the many corporate holiday parties, the club requests that comedians keep it clean. What "clean comedy" means could be an entire chapter of this book. In short, I'll say make sure that anytime you do any show, go out of your way to know what the guidelines are for your material. Keep in mind that not swearing and clean comedy is not always the same; you can definitely tell a dirty and inappropriate joke without swearing.

I hope you get real comedy-club stage time and have as much fun as I did my first time. It is an incredible experience. I showed up an hour and a half early for my first-ever Comedy Works performance and still forgot to hit record on my phone before going up. Thank goodness they were able to sell me the video of my performance. Hopefully, you have as much fun as I did, good luck!

My Denver Comedy Class

There is a notion in comedy of your comedy class, meaning the folks who, like a high school class, came of age at the same time as you. Six months in is premature to talk about this, but it does allow me to mention some up-and-coming local comedians, so I'll do it anyways. But first, how do we measure comedy class?

Using the New Faces contest might be a good checkpoint to determine comedy age in Denver.

New Faces is an annual contest for Colorado residents that in 2018 ran from spring to fall because there were so many entrants. There were so many that they also limited the contest to active participants in the New Talent Night program. All those participants competed in a series of events that culminated with a single winner (Mike Hammock).

There were fourteen nights of quarter-final shows. Each show saw twelve comedian competitors perform five-minute sets, and three from each show advanced to the semi-finals. Deacon Gray coordinated the contest, which was measured with scorecards that tallied originality, callbacks, and other comedy metrics.

A wildcard round offered three more new-talent comedians entry into the semi-finals. The semi-finalists got to perform six-minute sets twice, once at the suburban Comedy Works club, and once at the Downtown Comedy Works club. One winner was selected from each show and moved on to the finals, where seven-minute sets were performed.

Might New Faces work as a way to measure comedy class? If so, comedians who joined the community after the 2018 contest started, would be part of the 2019 class. Although it seems promising it is not the best measuring stick.

In addition to a lack of record keeping, transplants muddy the water. If it is your first year in Denver, but your fourth in comedy, what happens? Does it matter if you graduated from a smaller scene to Denver? What if you took the more unusual but not unheard of move from a larger market to Denver?

Perhaps this needs a less rigid approach.

A more subjective way to measure a rookie comedy class is to look around an open mic when there are less than ten people left to perform. When it is late and folks are yawning. If there is a person in that group whose entire set you can predict before they start, if you could go up in their place, and do their material, they are probably your class.

I'll use that measurement, and mention some local talent. None of them are household names today, but might they be in the future? I hope so! Let's go Denver!

I'll start with the transplants, these are people who when they arrived, I was lucky enough to be at their first mic. When they said they were in from out of town, I made a point to say hi, offer to answer questions, and be sure they knew what a great warm community we have here. I also made it clear I was brand new and had almost no idea what I was doing.

I remember meeting Mike Coppolino, and his Ron Jeremy bit. He is kind of hard not to remember. Mike came from the San Diego scene. Months after meeting him I was listening to a podcast episode (Art of Bombing, Big Frog, 20:35) and he was mentioned in the podcast. When not at open mics, Mike does street comedy, which I'm still not entirely sure I understand, but I think it's like busking. He is a seasoned comedian. He started a workshop mic for longer-form sets (ten to fifteen minutes), which I admire. I think it's great whenever anyone gives back to the scene like that.

I definitely remember meeting George Delgado at Voodoo Playhouse, a transplant from Las Vegas. He has good stuff and is a lot of fun to watch on stage. Once during a crowd-work open mic, he was adored by the crowd for moving fast and taking no prisoners as he moved through the audience. I had just been in Las Vegas when we first met so it was fun to trade stories about Las Vegas open mics from venues like the Jackpot Lounge and Silver Nugget Casino.

There were other transplants that quickly integrated themselves into the community without a welcome from me, but it wasn't long before we met.

Michelle Herring was originally from Colorado but moved back here from New York City. We would have writing sessions before mics sometimes which were fun and helpful. She ascended quickly and got a guest spot on a show with Sam Tallent, then got busy with work and life and took a break. People come and go, which is maybe why it's hard to know who is in your class.

Sarah Benson moved to Denver from upstate New York and her incredibly bubbly persona won over audiences instantly. I recruited her to be on one of my small shows, and she has been regularly booked on other shows since her arrival.

Then there are the folks whose comedy origin story began in Denver, at the noisy dive bars I have come to find endearing.

Louis Jesse Ricardo Martinez is mentioned in a few places elsewhere in this book. A gregarious and outrageously funny performer, I found out that he has been at this game over a year and a half, but has yet to enter a New Faces contest. His first mic ever was at the Comedy Room Room at El Charito, which is now out of business. Even cherished venues can quit the comedy scene it turns out.

Along with Josh Grambo, Louis runs a new open mic at 5280 Lounge in North Denver. Von Sprecken is the only other newer comedian I can think of, who has tried to start an open mic. Von Sprecken's mic briefly ran at Lincoln St. Station but died off when that venue closed down.

Miljen Aljinovic, sometimes known as "sad Bob Ross" when his hair is longer, is definitely the local comedian with the hardest-to-understand last name. His sets often come from an immigrant's perspective, I find them to be book smart, and often political, and enjoy how they often make you think.

Brian Evans came from Detroit and has a great bit about Denver's skyrocketing rent costs. He once gave me feedback on a set which I always appreciate. He traveled to Chicago to do stand-up and it was fun to hear about that adventure.

Phil Corridor is hilarious in a stoner, sleepy kind of way. He has yet to enter the New Talent program because he can't remember to call in. I love his stage presence and his consistent voice on stage.

Those are some of the up-and-coming local comedians I have run across in my first hundred mics in Denver. They are just a small sampling of an influx of new talent that shows no current signs of slowing down. Of course half of them may have quit by the time you read this.

Such is the nature of open mic comedy.

My Denver Comedy Class

My Denver Comedy Elders

I am one of the older folks you will find at a dive bar on a weekday around midnight angling for stage time. But I am still a little tiny baby when it comes to comedy knowledge and experience.

I am so old I was once asked at an open mic if I was the father of a stand-up comedian mentioned below. Because I was laughing hard at his jokes. I'm not sure which of us should be more disappointed.

One of my favorite things about these first six months is hanging around great comedians that inspire me to work harder with their hilarious talent.

Seasoned pro's like John Novosad, Sam Tallent, Brent Gill, Adam Cayton-Holland, Mitch Fatel, Al Jackson, Mike Stanley, Nancy Norton, Dr. Kevin Fitzgerald, and Brandt Tobler have inspired me with laughs, occasional conversations, and by being working professionals in a field I aspire to work in.

I also love being pushed by folks on the verge of becoming seasoned professionals, folks like Janae Burris, Alan Bromwell, Christie Buechle, Jose Macall, Derrick Stroup, Zac Maas, and Nathan Lund.

Then there are the folks who I regularly see at open mics that get me excited, because I know watching them work out their material will make me laugh. Folks like Ben Bryant, Michael Isaacs, Ben Duncan, Allison Rose, Austin Black, Nic Dean, Derek Walton, and Sammy Anzer. The comedians who are half my age but more than twice my senior as comedians really surprise me when they make me genuinely laugh, like Evan Johnson, Grayson Knight, and Roger Stafford.

If you can find great, hilarious, smart comedians to surround yourself with, do it. Go see them perform at traditional comedy clubs, showcases, and open mics. Soak it in. If you have a question about anything comedy, they probably know the answer.

The folks who run open mics deserve special credit, too. Not listed already, and also incredibly funny are Byron Graham, Roger Norquist, Caitie Hannan, Orin Be, Matt Cobos, and others. I can't overexpress my enthusiasm for this often thankless role in the comedy ecosystem. Hosts are the true heroes of the scene.

While putting the finishing touches on this book I took an additional step in soaking in knowledge from my elders. I reached out to a few kind souls who took time out of their schedules to generously share their wisdom.

Let's meet them! I will call them the transplant, the elder statesman, and the comedy-club owner. Keep reading to learn from them.

The Transplant

There are many hilarious transplants to the Denver scene, but one of my favorites is Michael Isaacs. Many folks would describe him as an alt-comic, but I think he is just funny. Damn funny. I still remember the first time I saw him perform. He was talking about chickens, and I was laughing my ass off.

My favorite thing about Michael is that he is generous and thoughtful as a community member. Anytime I have a question or need some advice, he is available. He was the first comedian to ever approach me with a tag idea for one of my jokes. More often than not at open mics, he is the most senior attendee watching the struggling comics.

We talked one day for almost two hours and it felt like ten minutes.

Michael started his comedy career in Chattanooga, Tennessee the first week of 2016. He was gushing when describing the scene. Funny comics, proximity to other major markets, like Atlanta and Knoxville, and his favorite bar in the world (JJ's Bohemia) rounded out his highlights.

He told me he did well at his first mic, better than the mics that followed. He believes that a fight-or-flight instinctual process can make you funnier, and it may have helped at that performance. He likes to bring a scaffold of a joke to stage and force himself to be in the moment and to express a new creative thought. His first-ever joke was heavily scripted though, it ended with him lighting a cigarette on stage, which he cringes at today.

There were about fifty comedians in his scene, with a little more than half of them regularly active. There were only two open mics a week and in the beginning, he wrote new stuff every week to see what would stick.

If he could time travel back to when he was just starting, he would tell himself to not be afraid of embarrassment and to not worry about looking cool on stage. He would tell himself to not have a precious attitude about jokes and to keep churning. He says he got this idea of not protecting yourself, which can turn off an audience, from Tim Heidecker.

He listened to a lot of podcasts before he got on stage for the first time, from big-name, national comedians. He learned from them that anyone can be a comedian, that the people who are successful were just people who tried it and stuck with it. Now he knows what he didn't then, that those podcasts have a lot of advice for touring comedians, but the advice does not always apply to new comedians. Still, they were formative for him.

One of his favorite audio experiences learning about comedy was listening to the audiobook Born Standing Up, read by the author, Steve Martin. He also thinks every aspiring comedian should listen to as many comedy albums as they can.

After a visit to Denver, he decided to relocate here. He chose Denver because it was smaller than major markets like Chicago, New York, and Los Angeles. Other similar markets to Denver we discussed were Austin, Minneapolis, Cleveland, and Atlanta. He likes just about everything about the Denver scene except its lack of a major media scene, which limits professional writing opportunities.

He moved to Denver with two other comic buddies in mid-2017. His other buddies have since quit the scene, but he struggled through the late nights and finally started getting noticed after about five months. People started talking to him, inviting him to shows, and more. His first mics were at Goosetown Tavern and Lion's Lair, which he described as intimidating then, as it is today.

Moving to Denver was the right choice for him.

"Denver is perfect, you can get stage time every night, there are plenty of showcases, people are actually good about paying people out here, but it's not the amount of pressure and that visibility, it's a little isolated, no other big cities within five or six hours."

"What that does with the Denver scene is it turns it into an incubation chamber where everyone knows each other and kind of pushes each other to get better. So when I see Ben Duncan slay it at some show I'm like I need to be working harder. I like getting to see your friends get better and people are really supportive, I've really enjoyed my decision so far, and there is Comedy Works, which is one of the best clubs in the country."

I asked him if this was a stepping stone for him and he deferred any talk of that. He wants to get better on stage over the course of years, and he pointed out that some nationally touring comedians are now making the case you can live in Denver and with the big airport you can get anywhere pretty easily.

He has done shows nearby in Boulder (about forty minutes from Denver) and Ft. Collins (about seventy minutes from Denver). We spoke at length about Denver's location for an aspiring touring comedian, and why you might want to get away from Denver, too.

"There is a pretty good tradeoff of shows with Denver and the surrounding areas. I've been to New Mexico a couple times and Texas. Those are long commutes but a very valuable learning experience, in the beginning, it is just going to be grueling, long, maybe not ideal drives, but it's important to get out to those new markets and have fresh ears on stuff that maybe has become stale to the people listening in your hometown."

"Everything is up for grabs, anything in your arsenal is able to be used. I'd like to experiment in the next year or two and do a long long run of twenty-five days in a row. Really hone those things without local fatigue, not that comics think that way at open mics but if you want genuine laughter you need genuine surprise, which is probably the most important thing. If people have heard it before, the level of appreciation is different, they are appreciating on a level of craft or what it was, versus really just being engaged in a temporary new form, which is the most exciting thing about jokes."

Michael's first six months in Denver differed from mine. He had prior experience. He also hit that next level of success, getting invited onto shows, faster than I did. I asked him what he was proud of from his start in Denver, and with some resistance from humility he finally shared:

"In the first six months you start learning the good shows in town, who's running those shows, people you respect and stuff like that ... it took me a good six months for people to have seen me and to see me do fairly well, but once that started happening in the first year after that I've gotten on those shows I wanted to get on, which means people are responding in a good way, people I respect. It definitely feels good, I'm really surprised at how the amount of stage time Denver allows me to get on a subconscious muscle memory level ... how comfortable I've gotten on stage which is almost more important than having a great joke, and how you present that joke, and having the crowd comfortable with your presence, and not weird that you're on stage in a context that is the weirdest context, like hey let's listen to this guy for a while."

"If I had known the strides that I would have made since moving here and getting on to shows I respected, and getting to semi-finals in New Faces I think I would have been really proud of myself right now."

I also tried to pull some downsides to the Denver comedy scene out of him. He was reluctant to say much negative which is just his personality, but he did speak on the topic. Even if he spun any downside as an eventual upside.

"As soon as you get inundated with the size, and the pain of waiting so long for time in a bigger scene as opposed to the smaller scene that I came from, how unimportant you are, more of a lesson, once you get past that it makes you stronger. I don't care if I have a bad set because there is always going to be another chance ... maybe the biggest disadvantage of the scene is you know nobody, at just a few years in--unless you have just a great flexible job--has plane trip money, so having to actually, if you're going to go to another market, which isn't bad, road trips are great, but you have to consider seriously, is my car in a good enough condition to make it that far? It becomes a trip versus in the south you can go to Atlanta for the night and come back that night, but it kind of makes this isolated incubation chamber, which raises the tides for everybody that everything is so highly pressurized here."

He continued on about how good Denver is for up-and-coming comedians.

"If you're able to run a joke ten times in a week, it could be totally different in a week and the people I admire are like that. I saw them three days ago and now it's totally different, but I know it came from the same seed. That definitely makes people get better quickly versus when I was back in Chattanooga. Yeah, you can go to a different city and try something out, but you can see people three times a week and if that's all the chances they have to get up, then they've number one had a four-day gap between telling it last time and this time, it's almost like they're not starting at point A again, if they had made it to point D, in terms of stage comfortability, and habits, they might be back to point C, you can just charge forward with it here."

I asked him to talk about New Talent Night which is such a big part of the journey for any Denver comedian. Michael is a B comedian now, having passed Newbie and C stages already. His next goal in the system is to host a New Talent night, and to perform and excel in New Faces again. A couple of times he emphasized how much he likes Comedy Works and the systems in place for newer comedians saying that "you know where you stand" with the club because of those systems. He emphasized that his knowledge of these systems is nothing he is expert on, so the below information is just what he has heard or experienced, and is subject to change.

"The system that Deacon Gray, New Talent Coordinator had set up, the first rung of that ladder is the newbie set in which really all he's looking for is that you're not going to throw up on stage or act like a maniac for two minutes. The stakes for that newbie set are pretty low. Once you prove that you're not a psycho you get put up to a C level, where you do three minutes, every eight to ten weeks."

"C set is four minutes every six to eight weeks. What helped me qualify for B level was advancing to semifinals in the New Faces competition and having strong performances at the C rung four or five times. Now I'm trying to hang out a little bit more (at Comedy Works), go to Thick Skin ... B (comedians) are asked to host New Talent night once they've shown it's something they are capable of. Comedy Works looks for how versatile they are as performers, can they not just do a set, can they host for you, not just being an oddball character on stage, being a host you're the anchor between the freaks they're going to see tonight, you are the normalizer between the freaks, resetting."

I asked him to dig into the New Faces competition a little more and he shared some of the inside scoop from his semifinal run in 2018. The order of comedians is based on a random selection process where the comics pull a number out of a bucket.

"You have some really, really strong comedians on there, the lineup for one week gets balanced, then it's really intense competition, Deacon Gray and John Toll alternated hosting. You want to pull the sweet spot of energy at person number five, at twelve everyone is tired, if you are going up on stage at Comedy Works you are going to get hit with a lot of stares and a lot of energy if you do well, there are nerves, especially on a stage that harnesses so much energy".

Michael advanced to the semi-finals, which he talked about more.

"The second round is at the South club and the Downtown club, so two weeks for semi-finals, same line up each time. My week Derrick Stroup advanced at the South club first. He still performed at the next round at the Downtown club. He got the shotgun spot, he got number one and if he could have won twice, he would have won twice. He destroyed right out the gate. The advantage of advancing from the first round is stage time at Comedy Works. There's nothing better than being on that stage, it's nuts. If you're able to crack that audience you're hit with a tidal wave."

I asked him if he had any advice for comedians at the six-month mark.

"Keep your head down and do well at mics. At the five or six month mark, I noticed a real difference in people noticing me". He also encourages comedians to be "supportive of people who aren't quite as far as you, (it means a lot when) anyone that's farther, that shows some cordiality or compassion when you're coming up and trying to find your legs."

I asked him what happened to his friends that moved out with him, and if there were any lessons there. They dropped out of the scene right before he started seeing success. Room Room is the Comedy Room Room at the now-shuttered El Chorito.

"At Room Room, you might go up forty-eighth, that disheartened them a little bit … learning to have fun at open mics and not worrying that much about your position, paying attention to other people develop and getting to know the people in the scene (is important). You can learn from seeing the misses, too. There is a point when your capacity for laughter at an open mic fills up but learning to watch in different ways … watching the audience and how they react or how the performer performs, shifting your perspective … this is a great opportunity to learn."

We talked about Facebook briefly. Comedy won him over to get back on the social-media giant's platform.

"I did not have Facebook for a long time until someone told me I needed it for comedy … good for finding comedians in other markets, I don't post … (but it's good for) trying to get a show or open mic together, probably 70% of my show opportunities come from Messenger on Facebook."

Finally, I asked him if he had any goals in the future.

"I'd like to start a mic or show in a month, it's almost a form of community service to start a mic, the reason I haven't done it sooner is I think just recently I know enough people to support that, there are no shows without showrunners and there is no stage time without shows."

The Elder Statesman

Aaron Maslow was a 2018 New Faces finalist and is an off-and-on nine-year veteran of open mic stand-up comedy. He started in Denver, where he did what he described as three years of unproductive comedic exploration. When he moved with his wife and kids to Edmonton, Canada he started getting serious.

After two years there and another two in Minneapolis, he returned to Denver in 2016 and found an almost completely turned over talent pool. Many comics had given up and some had moved on and up to touring.

He dove in and made sure to befriend new comedians he saw had talent and collaborated with them, in an effort to push and motivate himself. Today he runs and appears on showcases around Denver, hosts the only Saturday night comedy open mic in town, at Niccolo's Pizza, and does regular B sets at Comedy Works' New Talent Night.

When we talked about Denver as a market for up-and-coming comedians, he emphasized how many of our comedians came from elsewhere.

"You almost don't want to be a big fish in a small pond, you get this itch, I gotta get out of here, you can grow as a comic … Talk to anyone who has moved here from Omaha, Des Moines, the Midwest, there is no reason to stay there, you might get thirty minutes at a club a week."

Sometimes people move here from larger markets.

"If you've been to a bigger market, like look at a Mike Stanley, he was in Chicago and then moved here, he's like, here's a middle market I can work my way through on my way to being a bigger name somewhere else."

I asked him about Denver comedians moving to larger markets and he offered this note of caution.

"Christopher Titus said on the Comedy Works podcast that you don't go to L.A. unless you have two hours, and even then you don't stay there."

We talked about other markets too.

"Denver, Portland, Austin, Minneapolis, there are a handful, Atlanta, from all I've heard, those are destinations for small-market comedians who wanna grow up before they go to Chicago, New York, L.A. But in my opinion, it's like why would you go to the coast unless you have other things? You should already be established, you should have a show or credits."

With Aaron's long view I was curious how the popularity of comedy today compared to the scene he has experienced over nearly a decade.

"This is the most people I've ever seen. From what I've read it's a boom right now, it's on par with the eighties. I think the exception is there aren't as many new clubs being established but that comes with the advent of the access of comedy on the internet, you don't need to have a club to find comedy. Netflix, just about everybody seems to have a special, people you've never heard of, certainly more people think they have a skill and they wanna come and try it and get the accolades 'Oh you're so brave, you tried comedy.'"

Aaron doesn't even consider himself a comedian because he doesn't do it full time and professionally, but I asked him about his start anyways.

"Right as I started, which was December 27, 2009, my first time at a place called Bender's, it was a mixed mic at a music venue, now it's called Black Box, it's in Capitol Hill. I went in there, I had a few friends that came with me because I'd been talking about it for a long time ... it was horrible".

Aaron avoided Lion's Lair in the beginning, he didn't go for an entire year, even though he knew about it from that first night.

"I didn't go for the first year because I thought it was more serious ... didn't want to be in that network, I didn't want to embarrass myself in front of people who were doing it."

I asked him what he might tell himself if he could go back and mentor himself at the start.

"Be more invested early on ... I was two years in before I started calling in for New Talent Night, I should have gone full-in instead of half-ass, the first three years were unproductive."

On what he should have been doing:

"You get this regimen, you know what you are doing every week, it's ok, you get bored a little bit you take a day or two, but you get in with the community, support it, go see people who are better than you ... it's like exercise, I'm not going to get into any kind of shape exercising intermittently."

Aaron describes the Denver scene, New Talent Night, getting into the major club, as a "grind you have to commit to." He is committed to it now. He says being aware of your ability is key to your development, you have to be honest with how good you are, how much time you can do, and push yourself to improve if you think you are better than you are, you won't progress.

We talked a lot about the plight of the newer comic in the open mic scene. He thinks newer comedians sometimes get too focused on their new written material and miss the forest for the trees. Sometimes circumstance requires a deviation from your plan, which you need to learn to embrace. You need to give the room what it needs, even when it isn't what you hoped you might do that night.

"It seems like you're not working on what you came to work on but there are so many skills in performance arts that you have to develop ... Most of the time, in the beginning, you're going to be in shitty rooms with bored people, you need to approach it with I'm just going to be funny right now, that sets you apart, hosts notice, this guy is getting it, then they put you up a little earlier next time, that's what I look for, I want to see people who are willing to take chances ... (an important skill is) being able to call it and say I'll get another shot to work at these jokes, but now I'm gonna talk to the crowd and relate to them."

Inevitably you will fail, over and over, and when the going is not good, Aaron has advice.

"It's good to just be happy with your performance because sometimes people aren't in the mood."

Aaron credits his preparation and organization this second time through Denver's scene. When he got back he says he did things differently.

"In 2016 I could immediately pinpoint who was awesome and I made it a point to hang out with them. I saw who had potential ... being collaborative with people who constantly improve and who when they are performing, show they are improving ... we all know how jokes work but they try something new and you can see it work because they put a lot of time in before they got to stage, that's the mark of a really good comic, they put the work in before they get to stage."

In a dark turn, when discussing those who quit, we touch briefly on mental-health issues. He mentions that sometimes you don't notice when people drop out, and oftentimes, those who do "get sick" ... "that happens a lot." The conversation turns back to those comedians who do well and how they push him.

"I learn a lot from watching pros, there is so much more growth, the joke style is very creative, you can't have a bunch of setup-punchline for longer sets."

I asked Aaron what he has read or listened to that has helped him and he is emphatic about how good George Carlin's book Last Words is, and describes Mr. Carlin as one of the best comedic minds of the last one hundred years.

He speaks to the magic of comedy.

"The great trick of comedy is it's seemingly on the spot. As there is more access to comedy, that starts to go away, which is unfortunate. The audience knows you're not making that up on the spot. It's really important not to pull the curtain back too far when you are talking to a general audience, like magicians."

When I ask him for a concrete example he relates a personal experience.

"Don't call attention to the fact you forgot something, it breaks the illusion in a longer set, don't use a set list ..."

We end the conversation with some closing nuggets that will help any comedian, Newbie or regular at Comedy Works.

- "The sweet spot for a joke is once you tell it fifty to a hundred times."

- "Being organized is important."

- "Keep working on existing material, don't always do new stuff."

- "Always have a goal when you go to an open mic."

He ends with some advice for Denver open mic comedians.

"A lot of what counts is being seen and reliable ... to be present. It's not just doing your best open mic, you should be a nice person and a good part of the community."

The Comedy Club Owner

Wende Curtis is the owner of Comedy Works, Denver's premier comedy club. When I reach out to see if she will talk to me, she is easy going and makes herself available on short notice. I am surprised and impressed. Meeting with her is a bit of a thrill for a comedian at my level. After listening to all fifty of her "How Comedy Works" podcast episodes it felt like I knew her and her story from a distance.

We meet at the Comedy Works corporate office.

For the unaware, Wende started as a cocktail waitress at a Comedy Works location that no longer exists. She later was a club manager, and eventually became part owner of the downtown Denver club. She then took over complete ownership and expanded the club to a second suburban location south of Denver. She is an influential member of the Denver business community as well as the national comedy community.

It is obvious in our conversations how deeply she cares about comedy, the community, and in particular about the recently deceased Deacon Gray. Deacon was his stage name, Wende refers to him by his real name, David, sometimes during our conversation.

We discuss the 'How Comedy Works' podcast and whether it might come back or whether there was more information to distribute. She doesn't think so.

"We felt like we said what we needed to say ... the mission of the podcast was to relay information to our young comics in Denver and what we found was it reached a lot more than that."

In an emotionally charged conversation, because of Deacon's passing, we talk about the future of New Talent Night, Comedy Works' legendary program for up-and-coming comedians. Her commitment to the program is clear, but the details of what it might look like going forward are less so.

"We have a few ideas, probably be one person heading it up, one comic heading it up, with a hand full of comics working for him. David was unique because he didn't travel a lot and tour and that's difficult to find ... and then that love for teaching and the love of the craft and that art form. He was pretty unique in ways like that."

"A new person may be heading it up and maybe there is a group of four or five comics, and one of them would always be there but you can't just have four or five comics, but someone has to be the dad or the mom, you can't just leave the teenagers out there with the toddlers, that's gonna be a mess."

"We need to look at a couple different ways, this is what we need for the club, and this is what you need as a comic, which is a little more global."

"It needs to be an artist, someone who has been in the trenches and I know a lot of club owners take on that role ... but I don't think that's the answer ... I think it involves an artist, a stand-up comic, someone who's been there, not someone sitting on this side of the business."

"With two hundred employees and a gazillion comics and two locations, and seats to fill every night, my hands are really full."

Wende relays some touching stories about how organized Deacon was, even in his personal life, and how that became more apparent as she helped with his care when he was very sick.

"I took care of his business, did laundry while he was still here, drawers so organized, (he was) meticulously organized at many different levels."

Despite that organization, the New Talent Night was not left with a succession plan in place.

"My gut instinct is to prepare, to fasten down and batten down the hatches, but when it came to this ... I couldn't say to him hey we gotta get this together two years ago so that when you die the business is OK."

The result is that in 2019 there will be no Funny Final Four, a springtime comedy competition. Although nothing has been announced yet about New Faces for 2019, Wende thinks it will happen.

"The contest is coming up, that contest ... Susan our marketing director did it and it ran for a month in the summer, then Deacon came on, then it got bigger and bigger and now it starts in the spring and ends in the fall right before the holidays because there are that many contestants and it is so stinking cool."

I ask Wende why her business invests so heavily in New Talent Night when other club owners do not. When we talk about other club owners who are not investing in up-and-coming talent, she is passionate.

"... spoke volumes to me about who I thought they were and what their agenda is, to not add in any way to the rainforest but simply take, because (they're) not thinking about sustainability or the future or the right thing, not thinking about what they can do ... (just) what they can make."

She speaks about how the program is a service to the comedy community and why it has value to her.

"I need ... (performers) ... I use them every night of the week and in two locations and I need a variety ... anything I can do to help grow those ... (performers) ... quicker."

Wende is aware that comedic development happens elsewhere, too. There are open mics and showcases all around Denver. She credits Adam Cayton-Holland with really pushing for high-quality shows outside the club, which to the surprise of her industry peers, she encouraged.

"They are out there developing all over, don't get me wrong, there is no parent watching them in all those places ... hopefully, they are making good decisions on these stages, and they are going to get to my stage with a higher bar quicker."

"It was really Adam Cayton-Holland that opened that floodgate, so somebody says, well, I can start this gig over here and this guy will pay me in beers or whatever and I can get my friends up ... and it's funny when they call themselves producers because they aren't producers, but it still is for the greater good."

If she could change anything about New Talent Night, it would be to expand its geographic reach.

"I would like to get New Talent Night to the south club again because we have been open for over ten years and I really just thought we would have two open mic nights ... they didn't really want to come south, I mean the comics ... that's odd to me, hmmm, you want to be part of the system, this system, but we give you another shot and you don't."

Her goal would be a monthly show at the south club for New Talent Night, but it is not finding traction yet. She speaks about how the New Talent Night program lets comedians advance, how they can use it to get work at her clubs, and her role in that process. She emphasizes consistency and speaks about how Josh Blue was so successful.

"For you to be seen on our stage and for us to witness your consistency … because I don't have time to keep track of people … I can listen to it in my car … I generally don't watch a video of New Talent Night. Most of the time I'll take three months of time, every Tuesday night for three months, to see a snapshot, that I hear. If I hear it again and again … You just have to stand around and listen, what the staff is saying, what the pros are saying, what the managers might mention in a recap … Josh Blue, I heard things very quickly … you hear things all over."

When I ask for advice for new comedians she says comedy mirrors her approach to business, and relays a story about a new website. She focuses on getting stage time and diving in. Then asking questions with the benefit of that experience.

"If you're still thinking about it you're not doing it yet … jump in and go to all of these open mics and get a feel and they are going to give you tips."

"I feel like that of all things, that this applies, and that with Standup if you've been thinking about it then you've got an idea about a couple of jokes and whatever, so go do it, so you know what you're talking about when you ask someone questions."

She said one of the most important aspects is to have "the discipline to stay at it."

Which leads to one of her warnings about comedy.

"Don't drink too much."

She emphasizes she has seen this one negative pattern too often.

"Mostly don't drink too much, too many people that take this lifestyle, it becomes this thing that they drink too much and whether its calories or alcohol or whatever, that's not what it's about."

She encourages anyone trying to make it in comedy to go see pro shows and to talk to more experienced comedians.

"They are doing what you want to do, absolutely doing what you want to do, I don't think anything can replace watching that. I didn't when I was building this business. I was reading management books, I was talking to other people in the business, other comics, other club owners in restaurants and nightclubs and comedy clubs. Nothing replaces that."

When comedians in the local talent pool excel and look to larger markets, Wende is conflicted.

The Comedy Club Owner

"No, I never want them to leave, but you get them ready, the little birds to fly ... it always changes, you think you have a really solid bench, but then some leave and it changes."

When I ask her about other clubs around the country that she thinks are run well, and might be worth a visit from aspiring comedians, she mentions Cap City in Austin (Colleen McGarr), Acme Comedy Co. in Minneapolis, Hilarities in Cleveland, the Marc Grossman clubs like Helium in Portland, and the D.C. Improv (Allyson Jaffe). She discusses how she stays in touch with club owners to find out important industry information like who is actually clean, who draws crowds, who is great to work with, and even food and beverage minutiae.

When I ask her about how comedy has changed and where it might be headed, she has strong opinions. We talk about shifting demographics and other changing industry trends. She sees echoes of the past in the current ubiquity of comedy, but thinks that live comedy will forever hold a special draw.

"There will always be those that are aging out, they don't want to go to Red Rocks anymore and wait for parking ... A&E's An Evening at the Improv in the Eighties ... really hurt stand-up comedy at the time, everyone had one, I could have had one, they kept pulling more money out of it, it just became mundane, there was nothing unique ... and that's what I think is happening with Netflix ... soon there is going to be a seven-and-a-half minute special because now there is a fifteen-minute special and they aren't special anymore, because when you can't name them all off, or at least get 80% of them, it's not special ... you have so much access ... of course on your computer and television ... but live is the exceptional piece that ignites my fire."

When I ask about her future Wende is content with where she is. She doesn't need to make a big splash with something radically different. She is considering writing a book but is modest about who would care.

After sitting with her and feeling her passion and enthusiasm for live comedy, my guess would be that a lot of people would care. And that she has a lot to be proud of in a business that is inspiring so many to experience comedy as an audience member or a performer on stage.

Comedy Podcasts and Books

I am so grateful for those who came before me and documented an incredible amount of content about comedy, in podcasts and books. Yes, you can watch video forever: stand-up specials, TV shows, sketch shows, documentaries and more. And I have. A documentary about Joan Rivers, a lecture from Ralphie May, Mr. Show, almost 4 hours of lecture from Ari Shaffir at the Comedy Store, and more.

But what I think has been even more important to my development as a comedian are podcasts and books. So I'd like to take some time to share what I consumed in my first six months. Hopefully this helps you save some discovery time.

Let's start with my favorite-ever comedy podcast, Let's Talk About Sets (letstalkaboutsets.com). I found it with an organic web search for comedy podcasts. Self described as a punchy podcast from NYC on the "science" and craft of stand-up comedy by comics who love it, it is exactly that.

It is smart, insightful, and full of references to great stand-up comedy. I like to listen to an episode and parse it for mentions of talented comedians, then download related comedy albums, and enjoy and study them. It is a gift that keeps on giving.

You can search their website for episodes by content. So if you want to deep dive into hecklers or roasts or almost any comedy subject matter, this is the podcast for you. I can hardly think of another podcast resource that was more impactful to me during my first six months than Let's Talk About Sets.

And it continues to have regularly released new episodes. As I write this, the latest episode features NYC (by way of Minnesota) comedian Geoffrey Asmus, who I met and spoke with at Lion's Lair when he swung through Denver in January of 2019.

Other podcasts in this category are You Made It Weird with Pete Holmes, and Good One: A Podcast About Jokes with Jesse David Fox, as well as the Art of Bombing.

I've enjoyed some episodes of The Church of What's Happening Now with Joey CoCo Diaz, who tells great road stories. I love hearing about his early times in Denver and Boulder, but this one is more like the talk show style podcast I mention below.

There are other good instructional podcasts that no longer generate new content but their archives of past episodes are still a goldmine of comedy information. You can still get value from, for example, Bombing with Mike Dorval. His episode with Gary Gulman is a gem. Everything with Gary Gulman is a gem; find anything and everything you can involving him. There are some great Gary Gulman episodes on the James Altucher podcast for example.

There are a whole slew of podcasts by comedians that are themed around topics that are not comedy. You can get entertainment from them and maybe pick up some ideas if you want to start a podcast yourself, but I didn't find them immensely useful. A good example is Timesuck, by Dan Cummins. Funny, yes. Instructional? Less so.

Then there are interview podcasts like the Joe Rogan Experience, which I think fall into the same category, except when the interview subject is a comedian. Then the podcast can have helpful content, like episode #1210 with Tom Papa. WTF with Marc Maron is another great one in this category.

There are talk-show-like podcasts that can teach you how to entertain by example, and often touch on comedy topics. A good example is The Brilliant Idiots which includes Andrew Schulz, who was an influential part of my comedy visit to New York City. He is hilarious.

I would like to give special mention to Green, a comedy podcast which is dense in material for starting out as a comedian. It is from two beginner NYC comedians, including Stu Melton, who I met at an open mic in Denver, during my first six months.

One of my favorite podcast pursuits is listening to local comedy podcasts. Even though the star power and production quality might be lacking, they make up for it with amazingly helpful local content.

Comedy Podcasts and Books

You can learn about shows, comedians, venues and all kinds of local information, which is incredible when you are just getting started. It's like having the best, smartest mentors in your ear, and they will talk to you anytime, when you are driving, when you are at the gym, even when you have insomnia.

I don't know how comedians got up to speed quickly on local scenes before you could listen to hundreds of hours of inside baseball on demand, but it must have taken a lot longer.

In no particular order, here are Denver comedy podcasts I have enjoyed. I got a lot of value from listening to Deacon Gray episodes. Although he is no longer with us, his masterful knowledge of joke writing and comedy lives on through the magic of podcasts. Some of these may be inactive by the time you get to them. I have marked the ones I know are inactive, but keep in mind, there is no reason not to plow through older episodes.

- Talkin' Shop with Anthony Crawford
- Sam Tallent's Half Hour Prophecy (inactive)
- My Dining Room Table with Adam Cayton-Holland (inactive)
- Left Hand Right Brain with J.D. Lopez
- InFauxMation with Brent Gill
- One on Lund with Nathan Lund (inactive)
- Joke and Destroy with Jeremy Pysher and Andres Becerril
- How Comedy Works with Wende and Rick

- My Favorite Episodes:
    - Sam Tallent (22)
    - Dr. Kevin Fitzgerald (39)
    - Christopher Titus (41)
- Schooling Noah with Aaron Maslow & a special guest

I am sure I have missed some other great podcasts, if you have a favorite, please share with me through the contact form on my website, www.markmasters.co.

Two last things: a quick shout out to Pocket Casts, my go-to podcast app on Android and the Web. Secondly, a pro-tip from Michael Isaacs, who says you should re-listen to good podcast episodes periodically through your comedy journey. As you develop you will take different lessons from them, and can get new value from them.

Books

Everyone learns in different ways and I tend to learn best from reading. I read a lot of books in my first six months because 2018 was a year I challenged myself to read fifty books. I ended up reading forty, covering many subjects.

Here are the books I read that covered comedy:

Born Standing Up - Terrific read from Steve Martin, comedy aside I would rate this a must-read book for anyone. The man is a genius, and this book is hilarious and poignant.

This Here Is Magic - Gets in on a technicality, this is actually a biography of a professional entertainer who is a magician, I loved the first half and it is a must read for anyone considering performance art as a hobby or career.

Mastering Stand-Up - This is the first book you should read in my opinion. Comedians love to crap on books and for good reason, you really do need to learn on stage in front of an audience, but if you have to start somewhere, this is as good a place as any.

How To American - I heard this Silicon Valley actor and comedian promoting this book on a podcast. Biography books by comedians get similar after a while but this was the first one I read. If you want to know more about how working at a strip club can help your comedy career, start here.

A Horse Walks into a Bar - This is a fiction piece that I didn't care for very much about a comedian in Israel. A little too weird for me. Probably I'm not sophisticated enough to get it.

Planet Funny - Interesting book by Ken Jennings, the Jeopardy champion guy. It covers how everything is funny now, even bank advertisements on TV. Not great for my fledgling stand-up career but well written and worth my time.

Zen and the Art of Stand-Up Comedy - I loved this book. You could replace Mastering Stand-Up with this one. By Jay Sankey, it covers the basics of being a comedian. It is very dated, even discussing how to mail VHS tapes, but it is quick, full of great insights that stand the test of time, and a fun read.

Food - After I met Jim Gaffigan, I got this as a library e-book and plowed through it. Easy, fast read that is basically a stand-up special in written form. Not good as instructional material.

I Killed - When people ask me what my favorite comedy book is, I say this one. I loved it. It is dozens of two-to-three page stories from working comedians who were asked to share their craziest road comedy story. I laughed, I cried, and I learned things. Read this one.

Poking a Dead Frog - If you want to be a comedic writer someday, this is a must read. I found it a little long winded sometimes, but I feel like it helped me as a writer. I think I was expecting it to be funnier. Probably something you could hold off on reading until year two plus.

Tragedy + Time - This Adam Cayton-Holland best seller moved me. I felt guilty borrowing it from the library since Adam is a Denver legend. It is wonderfully written and poignant about tragedy, while also covering why comedy is important to Adam and covers his beginning in the Denver comedy scene. Support local authors!

Still Foolin' Em - Billy Crystal's autobiography will make you cry and laugh, and it has great history and advice for comedians as small nuggets in an overall fun story. I'll give you my favorite nugget which was a story about Jack Rollins telling a young Billy that he needs to leave a "tip" in his performances to really be great. Which means he needed to tell more about himself and be more personal with audiences.

SeinLanguage - Very similar to Food by Jim Gaffigan but by Jerry Seinfeld. Fun if you are a Seinfeld fan.

Pryor Convictions - Richard Pryor's autobiography, excellent for students of comedy history, but not a lot of instructional information, and any industry information is a little dated. Still a great book by a legend.

The Humor Code - A very nerdy exploration of the science and anthropology of comedy by the C.U. professor with the benign violation theory of comedy, Peter McGraw. I Enjoyed the first half more than the second half. Maybe I got tired, or maybe I was less interested in international theories than domestic ones. My international touring days are far, far away.

I have read a few books after my six-month mark, that I have enjoyed, in particular, Comedy Writing Secrets. Have you read books that were good for you as a beginning comedian? Please share them with me.

Also a final note, that I paid for almost none of these books. The library is an incredible American institution. I wrote a lot of this book at public libraries. Here is a pro-tip, all libraries have an inter-library loan system, so if your branch or even your entire city library system doesn't have a book, ask a librarian if they can get it for you. I have received books from libraries from far, far away (Zen and the Art of Stand-Up Comedy), and have also requested the library system buy and stock their shelves with a book (How To American) and had the request approved! This is all free. Libraries are the best.

One Way To Gain Hosting Experience

For many years before this comedy adventure, I ran meetup events. I still do. Despite them being business oriented, one day a funny thing happened. I noticed that these meetups had some things in common with comedy showcases. Both were groups of people sitting in chairs listening to someone. I wondered, could one live inside the other?

When I tested this hypothesis I learned that meetup audiences can benefit from comedy, and I later validated this with audience surveys. In the other direction, performers benefit because they get access to quality stage time. And this is special stage time, it has a rare quality. It is in an environment that mimics corporate comedy work.

Best of all, for me, I got to experience running a show, which helped me because it allowed me to learn what I liked and didn't like from performers. Hopefully, I thought, I could use that practical knowledge someday when I am on a show lineup and leverage my discoveries to be easy to work with.

Something I did not anticipate might have been the best benefit. My efforts led to me having more and higher-quality stage time, that I controlled.

One Way To Gain Hosting Experience

So how did I get from having a crowd, to eventually regularly putting on shows within larger meetings that local comedian Aaron Maslow described as "an invaluable opportunity to practice for corporate comedy gigs"?

It all started with the first time, where my first obstacle was finding actual talent.

I loved the comedy of Nic Dean, a transplant from Omaha, who is a storyteller, and a really funny guy. I sheepishly asked him one night at a mic, if he would be willing to do five minutes at an event. Just like Nic, he said "hell yeah dude."

And then he told me I had to do some material too, which I hadn't planned on. He explained that would help get the audience ready for him.

The idea of me performing was personally helpful for two reasons.

First, it taught me that people need to be told it is OK to laugh and to be set into the right mood, for a comedy show to be most successful. This is hosting 101, but at the time I didn't know anything about it. There is a whole world of information relevant to the skill of hosting. Perhaps in a future book, I might cover that topic.

The other huge benefit of my performing was more stage time. At an open mic in my first six months, I was lucky to ever see an audience of ten people and a few minutes. If I was in charge, I could get the crowd as big as I was able, and do as much time as I wanted, within reason of course.

I bought a two-hundred-dollar DJ speaker set, which came with the speaker, a stand, a cable, and a cheap microphone. I upgraded the mic to a Shure (eBay) and got a free mic stand from a friend. I also bought one of those foldable canvas wagons which made it easy to transport my new portable comedy room set up.

The first show was a nice success and I have become a little more sophisticated since then about booking performers.

When I see a comedian who I think would do well at one of my shows, I give them a small flyer encouraging them to fill out an online form. It is a Google Form that asks for comedy biography information I can use in promotional materials as well as for introductions at the show. It is very similar to a form you might fill out for a comedy festival. Here is a clone of it so you can create your own, no need to fill this out: http://bit.ly/bookshowform

I want the talent to feel like they are getting more than just stage time out of a show I produce, and to know I am well organized.

I make sure the comedian knows I am promoting them online. I make sure to over communicate logistical details like where they have to be and when, and what to expect from the audience. When I can, I provide specific audience demographic information to the comedian, so they can best tailor their set list.

For many comedians, performing corporate clean is not second nature. This has been painful to learn, but I guess, hilarious too. Let's just say I have had a couple of unhappy audience members. I have learned that coaching comedians can help a lot.

I video record their performance and offer the comedian a copy of their set. I discard their video after and make it clear the video is not going to be published.

I once did a competition performance and later found out my set was streamed live over the internet without my knowledge or permission. I was upset and disappointed and have always remembered that feeling, and go out of my way to make sure performers know that I will not distribute their performance.

You might think that any exposure is good, but that isn't true. First, you want only your very best work to be public. Second, your jokes may someday be part of an act making you money or on a comedy album. It might be a little crazy to think you can monetize any material from your first six months, but if there is no obvious benefit, might as well err on the side of controlling your exposure.

I paid half a dozen performers while I was figuring things out. I was an outsider then and this helped me attract talent. Ideally, I would always pay, but logistically it is not always possible. I do always provide free drink or food to performers, out of respect for their time and skill. I keep in mind that I am providing valuable stage time in a unique environment, which is a commodity.

During a show, I do other normal show-running things. I run a timer, I flash a light, I get on the mic between performers. I tear down the equipment at the end of the night. In what is probably an uncommon activity, I do send a survey out to gather audience feedback. I use this to help curate what performances I will put on stage in the future. I have also used it to modify the number of performers and length of sets.

Since as a show host I do some material, I keep a log of the jokes I tell at every show and do my best not to repeat material when there is a chance of audience overlap.

Adding a comedy show to any event is a lot of hard work. It is very stressful. I have to please the performers, the venue, and the audience. Yes, I get stage time and experience, but I hope someday maybe I'll get one more thing out of it.

Selfishly I hope that someday, when I deserve it, someone who I have on one of my shows will invite me to their show. Or remember me when they need to help someone fill a spot.

One Way To Gain Hosting Experience

Seeing as I am writing a book called Not Good Yet, I imagine it might be a hot minute before that happens. And that's OK with me.

Not on Facebook

I am not on Facebook, which you already know if you read about the time I got up early at Lion's Lair by accident.

I think it is important to address this. I have my own personal philosophical reasons for not being on Facebook, and pragmatic ones, too. I'd rather spend my time creating content than getting lost in an addiction-fueled game of consuming content and keeping up with the Joneses.

I have had more than one comedian who learned about my Facebook aversion say something like "oh, that's why you are so happy."

But I've also had dozens say something along the lines of "that is a huge mistake" And those comics are right.

It is a real negative for me. Comedians use Facebook all the time to communicate.

If you can be on it and balance some semblance of positive personal psychology, terrific. You'll know when mics are canceled last minute, you'll have better luck networking with out-of-town comedians. You'll have a way to remember comedians during a conversation, by just plugging their name into Facebook and seeing a picture pop up immediately, and what friends you have in common.

When I have seen glimpses of success with comedy, which are rare in the first six months, I think many of them stem from me being stubborn. Like a runner training for a marathon who refuses to give up after a cramp, a low-energy day, or partially crapping their pants halfway through a training run, I am one persistent son of a gun (technically a son of a very hard-working immigrant and hard-working, amazing mother).

I rarely give up when I set my mind on something. Which in the case of Facebook may be to my detriment, but whatever, I've chosen my hill to die on, and I'm fighting this battle. At least if and when I make it, I can say I did it my way.

You may have picked up so far that I am lucky enough to travel on occasion. I like to use personal and business travel as an opportunity to practice my comedy craft. I find it very entertaining to participate in out-of-town open mics. All the material from other comedians is new, and my material is new to them. I learn about how jokes "travel", or in many cases, don't.

Traveling and finding shows is way harder without Facebook, but part of my quirky personality is that I just lean into the difficulty. Fine, I have to make in-person connections and get archaic phone numbers. Maybe I have to visit a city twice to get the same value someone on Facebook might get in one visit.

The reality is I'm not good enough yet to get on showcases regularly anyways, so I believe I'm not missing out on much. Maybe when I get better I'll change my mind about Facebook, who knows.

Also, in my six first months, I figure a social media presence can only hurt me, I don't need people knowing how bad I am. Might as well wait until I have some really good video.

So for now, I am not on Facebook, and maybe stop bothering the other Mark Masters from Denver. You can contact the real me through my website contact form at www.markmasters.co, I respond to all inquiries, usually the day they are sent.

Comedy Festival Visit

One of the things I was lucky to be able to do in my first six months of comedy was attend the Red Clay Comedy Festival, in Atlanta GA.

It was hilarious, rewarding, and instructional.

I was unexpectedly surprised by what a great learning experience it was to see dozens of incredibly talented comics, in such a short amount of time.

I was especially taken by the comics from New York who have a style of comedy I grew to enjoy. Quick punchy stories and liberal doses of crowd work sprinkled throughout their sets. Almost as if they were demanding attention from a crowd that just as easily could be watching the Yankees or Mets on a corner TV. In short, they grabbed your attention and held it, often masterfully.

I'll highlight a dozen or so of my favorite performances from the weekend.

But first, let's cover some logistics.

Cost? I paid less than a hundred dollars for a three-day VIP ticket that got me two headliner shows (Janeane

Garofalo and Ron Funches), access to twenty-five different shows, and fifty different comedians. Even a memorable acoustic performance by Mike Cooley of Drive-By Truckers at The Earl. What I'm trying to communicate is, this is a total steal for anyone who likes comedy. My ticket price even included a festival T-shirt.

The entire event takes place in East Atlanta Village, with a hipster vibe and plenty of great bars and restaurants. Comedy takes place in two tents (adjacent to [The Midway](#)) and three indoor venues, all within walking distance. [529 bar](#) and [The Earl](#) have professional stages ready for small concerts and perfect for comedy (although I personally didn't like the indoor smoking at 529 bar). [The Argosy](#) back room was the most visually interesting. Performers worked on the floor in front of folding chairs and an elevated bar seating area, surrounded by pinball machines (including some beautiful antiques) and the coolest wooden cephalopod structure I've ever seen, above them.

The organizers [Jennifer O'Neill Smith](#), [Mike Albanese](#), and [Gilbert Lawand](#) were as friendly and accessible as the comics. Being able to say hi and chat with someone who was recently on Conan, or Jimmy Kimmel, or Netflix was an unexpected surprise. Talking with other attendees about favorite sets and jokes added to the sense of community.

One last note before I get to the performers. Late night was always fun at the nearby Little Five Points area, and

Atlanta's quirky and fun sides shone on visits to the Clermont Lounge and Ponce City Market.

Without further ado, let's meet some of the characters that made my belly ache at the 2018 Red Clay Comedy Festival, in no particular order. I'll mention joke topics but do my best not to give away any punchlines.

Nathan Macintosh

New York-based comic, originally from Canada. I think if Nathan only spoke whatever it is they speak in Canada, and I couldn't understand it, I would still laugh. His voice modulation itself is funny. He made my sides hurt with his material on McDonald's and other mundane topics made ridiculously funny. He made me laugh and then kept his foot on the pedal until he said thank you and good night. I first saw him as the opener for Janeane Garofalo, and then again in a tent with about 20 people. This is a comic who has recently done 5 minutes on Conan. What an experience! The best compliment I can pay Nathan is that when he repeated a bit, I laughed just as hard the second time through. That's solid writing.

Kate Willet

Kate was the feature — that's fancy comic talk for the person before the headliner — for Janeane Garofalo, and she crushed in front of hundreds. Intelligent, but with a hint of raunch, she had the audience rolling with material about her life, sex, dating, the many inadequacies of men (with particular emphasis on men in the comedy community) and more. She has an episode on Netflix in the series The Comedy Lineup, with 15 minutes of her material. Very funny stuff. While having a beer at the Midway Pub she walked by and I was amazed that a comedian with material on Netflix was just hanging around. Then it got even more interesting. She did a closing-night set at the small tent with a couple dozen in the audience at most. Although she didn't seem as present and natural as she was in her element on a headlining-style stage, she was still ridiculously funny, with punchy material that showcased her skill in writing, timing, and using her voice to guide the audience to laughter. In her defense, I think either she had a flight to catch or the host made a mistake, he ran the comedians in top-down order, but I'm pretty sure she was supposed to close, not open.

Luke Mones

That someone who looks this young has been on stage at Caroline's, online at Funny Or Die, and is perhaps working on a Comedy Central show is impressive. As is his self-deprecating humor. Another New York-based comic, his ability to riff on stage when things go wrong (accidental house speaker music playing, for example) was funny. Although he joked he was too tall for comedy, his stories about retail, dating, and life in New York City without a lot of money earned him big audience laughs.

Kevin Yee

Did you like Avenue Q, but wish it had been gayer? Even if not, you'll still probably love Kevin Yee, who is as infectiously happy on stage as his musical performance comedy is ridiculous and over-the-top gay. Talented, funny and decidedly not safe for work, Kevin Yee was another New York stand out at Red Clay. He would like everyone to please watch his show on Hulu, by the way. Thank you for the family-planning advice Kevin, but I think I'll pass anyway.

Chris Scopo

Chris is from Queens and he won't like me saying this, but if you've ever peed your pants listening to a comedian who after many Atlanta craft beers looks and sounds like Mark Wahlberg, you have found him. His material about his parents and living with roommates in NYC was gold. Even better was how I watched him handle some rude, loud audience members. Like a true pro, he finished his bit for the rest of the crowd, before politely and then hilariously, forcefully putting them into their place. Let's just say they were quiet after he was done with them, and the crowd was dribbling even more beer onto the tent floor. It's pretty easy to find video of Chris online, check out his stuff at Laugh Factory.

Allison Rose

From Denver! By way of Kansas. Allison hosted the most popular open mic in Denver as judged by the number of comics who sign up. Seriously, no joke, I'm still waiting to be called up from last year (and since El Chorito went out of business I guess I'll be waiting a long time!). I've seen her perform around Denver and it was great to see her in Atlanta. Her material is personal and often dark, but my favorite was when she made a hilarious comparison between shopping for produce and a common experience for the American woman. Even though I'm not one, I laughed and it felt relatable all the same.

John Michael Bond

He lives in Los Angeles but is quick to point out he's there for reasons other than he got too big for his old scene. His marriage to his high-school sweetheart leads to most of his material, though he does have a crazy story about an animal that is super old.

Tom Delgado

Got to catch Tom twice during the festival, he lives in NYC and has funny observations about life there including rent and roommates and his disdain for long-distance running. He was once a lawyer.

Nathan Lund

Compiling this list I am struck by how NYC must be run over with web designers. Every NYC comic has a slick website. Even some of Denver's funniest like Nathan, don't have a dedicated website. But looks like he rules on Twitter. Nathan runs a great open mic in a Denver dive bar (3 Kings Tavern) with short sets. Nathan was outstanding in front of a weird crowd on the big stage at The Earl, one night of the festival. His jokes about alternative transportation and drug-taking animals hit with me but drew a tepid crowd response, which I thought was unfortunate. The comics sure liked him, I kept seeing him hanging with other comics including Ron Funches right after his headlining set. Go check him out live. He is a big teddy bear wrecking machine of fun and laughs.

Ryan Schutt

Hilarious. Great energy and crowd work to launch a great set about the real-estate industry (kind of), ice cream, and his time in Washington DC. His date story that he did in a longer set at The Argosy killed. Another very tall comedian who is now based in NYC, where apparently those types just grow on, very tall, trees. Also, an observation, Ryan is billed almost dead last on the festival poster, which means either he improved A LOT since his submission, he sandbagged, or somebody made a mistake. This guy is going places. Like an urban beach. [Edit: I noticed the bottom half of the bill is alphabetical by first name, so never mind]

Maria Wojciechowski

Man, I hope I spelled that right. Maria breaks the rule that all NYC comics have websites, but she's on the Twitter. And she's funny. A southern girl (Alabama) who is now in NYC, she weaves absurdist proclamations with stories about her Mom, her definitely-not-villainous boyfriend, and other family members like an in-law and grandpaw. Felt lucky to have caught her act in the small tent and The Argosy.

Jeff Koehn

Another Denver comic and he'd be the first to tell you, the most awkward of the four performing at Red Clay. But in a funny way! Jeff can do an impression as well as tell a structured joke, or have the audience dying over a one-liner that's always in a hurry to kill. I hear he did the rounds at Atlanta comedy clubs before and after the festival and hopes to tour the South in the future.

Christine Ferrera

If Jeff Koehn is awkward, Cristine Ferrera is a new level of comedic uncomfortable. With absurdist takes on dating, Starbucks drinks, and ice cream. She has a great website with a lot to check out, so click on her name.

Janeane Garafolo

Our first headliner and a nostalgic one, she was one of the first stand-up comedians I ever saw live more than 20 years ago. I haven't seen her live since but she's been in movies and on TV a lot. Similar but more chaotic energy this time and she replaced her notebook with what appeared to be a Ziploc bag of newspaper clippings. Her high-energy spirit was evident while she roamed the aisles of festival goers mid-set. Good to see you again Janeane. I like that she doesn't need a website. When I saw her first, websites did not exist, and now who cares because she's famous enough to have a top-Google-ranked Wikipedia page.

Ron Funches

It took me a while to figure out where I knew Ron's voice from, but at least I was laughing the whole time. He's Cooper in Trolls! Ron was great, partaking on stage between stories, and making the audience roll with laughter. He claimed to still be working on a bit about his Mom and a famous person, but it seemed pretty well polished to me, I just about lost it. Once you get super rich Ron and put that plan in action, don't forget about Red Clay and our good times. Ron has the best adult-child laugh I've heard in a long time, check him out and you'll see what I mean.

Bob Place

An Atlanta comic who would excel at the Denver institution "the wrongest joke," Bob weaves dark, gross stories with foul twists and laughs that shock and amuse. I'm sure he'd be funny, but you probably don't want to sit near him on an airplane.

Geoff Tice

Another Denver comic, a regular at Comedy Works south (and downtown I presume, but I'm not sure how he fits on stage) Geoff stood tall and slung jokes at The Argosy and smoky 529 bar. Don't ask him about his name unless you want to laugh but do ask him about his engagement, it's hilarious. I hear that Geoff made the art on the festival T-shirt. He is as talented a graphic designer as he is a comic, based on show posters I see around the Denver comedy scene.

Trey Dunn

Trey is an Atlanta-based comic but I could have mistaken him for a New York comic, his stuff was so polished and well constructed. Whether he was getting laughs with back humor, or perhaps the world's most boring job, he had the audience in stitches both times I saw him.

Kenny Deforest

Less than a year since Late Night with Seth Meyers, Kenny from Brooklyn via Missouri slayed as the feature comic before the Mike Cooley concert. What impressed me the most was his closing bit which was heartfelt, personal and rife with ... tragedy. Yes, it was funny, but it educated, too. I've heard it said that traditional humor is dying in favor of [Nanette style comedy](). I feel this is an overreaction, but hearing a kind of similar story told in person, when you can look the storyteller in the eye, I better understand the appeal. The future may look less smiley in comedy rooms if this comes to pass. But it won't be void of value, Kenny taught me that a brilliantly timed trage-story can provoke laughter and simultaneous deep introspection. Thanks for sharing that story, Kenny.

My experience at Red Clay was formative for me as a young comedian, I encourage anyone who can to find a comedy festival they can attend. If cost is an issue, offer to volunteer. Do your best to make some out-of-town connections for places you may travel in the future. A comedy festival can be an incredible learning experience.

Comedy-Mecca Visit - New York City

Traveling from Colorado to New York City for comedy tourism is a thrill. With big eyes as a still-wet-behind-the-ears comic, I aspire to find my way onto a stage and see some shows. The story of my trip reflects a time when I am new and fresh and eager, visiting what is definitely a magical comedy town.

When I arrive I am in awe of everything. So noisy, so busy, so crowded.

But this subsides.

After a couple of days I walk by Spider-Man, dangling upside down aside hundreds of film crew milling around Penn Station, and I don't even gawk. I barely glance. Not because seeing Peter Parker in a superhero suit isn't incredible, but more because of the incredible things I have experienced over the last 72 hours.

I land at Laguardia at 1 p.m. on a Tuesday. I make it to a 3 p.m. open mic at Otto's shrunken head, hosted by Jimmy Peoples. One of the comics tells a story about bartending at a Chinese restaurant. He tells a story about Louis C.K. coming in for takeout. Louis has a water at the bar while he waits. The comic debated talking to him, his deliberations are funny, he eventually decides against engaging. Louis leaves after dropping a twenty dollar tip for the water. A famous comedian story! New York City delivers already. Little did I know it could get better. Much better.

One of the fun things about being a new comic is the constant learning. Like with any new craft, in the beginning, your experience is chock full of lessons. Once you get pretty good at something, you keep learning and evolving, but the frequency of lessons learned goes way down. Where you put yourself can also impact how you learn. On this trip, my experience level combined with New York City sends my learning through the roof.

A comic in Denver once said to me on observing my corny and eager attitude, "looks like you are still having fun, that's cool". Many more seasoned comedians I see in Denver seem to be having less fun, they seem worn down by the grind. Worn down by a system where advancement and success can be driven by luck.

I don't personally have that feeling yet though, I'm climbing rungs nearly every day. Everything is fun still. Eventually, the learning curve will break, and this whole pursuit might become a more boring grind. But for now it is an express subway train of learning.

Two lessons smack me in the face during my five minutes on stage in Manhattan at Otto's.

First, I learn that riffing and being "real" can be way better than scripted material. Robot voice is what Bill Burr calls the opposite of what you want to do as a stand-up comedian. Even after you have told the same bit hundreds of times, the audience wants to hear it like it's the first time you ever said it, like it's coming off the top of your head.

I am halfway through my set, pretty solid robot voice going for me when something different happens. For context, I've done fifty or so open mics at this point. Enough to have some idea what I'm doing, but mostly enough to have crushed any dreams I'm a savant that won't have to work at this. Enough to know that I am not good yet.

The first half of my set got some polite laughs. I know by now the difference between a civilian laugh and a comic's laugh. Even worse is a polite comic's laugh. It isn't so much supportive as it is a dagger delivering a message. I see what you are trying to do with that, but I know, in real time, several ways to do that better. You suck at this, have you considered giving this up? It can be pretty harsh, the polite comic's laugh.

I launch into a bit that relies on an outrageous story title in the New York Times. It gets a half chuckle, which my lizard brain misinterprets as laughing at the mention of the New York Times.

Reviewing the recording, I later realize the chortle was for the story title. But in my head, somehow, in real time, I come up with and spit out "yeah, it's true … we have the New York Times in Colorado". This self-deprecating, absurdist, and clearly off the cuff take earns a couple (small) real laughs.

Lesson learned, be real, be in the moment, and you can earn laughs even from a hardened crowd.

The second lesson I learn is about jokes traveling. Jokes don't have tiny suitcases exactly, but some maybe have ankle bracelets, meaning they are restricted to a pre-defined geographic area.

When I try to tell a geographically constrained joke, disaster strikes. I see my mistake coming about ten seconds before it unfolds for the audience. It is like a Saturday morning cartoon slowed down car crash sequence. With my robot voice in full gear and thinking a couple of lines ahead I realize my regional reference to a not very fancy Denver grocery store, is not going to work.

I am already committed to the bit. What choice do I have? I plow ahead. I fumble awkwardly through the joke, look like a two-bit idiot, small-town hack, and take my lumps. But I make a mental note to always double-check my material in the future when going up on stage out of town.

A few comics later Otto's is a wrap, so where next? Most of the comics leave to hit their service industry jobs, one with a big GrubHub bike food bag around his neck.

I ask a comic on the way out what other mics to hit, and he mentions the Grisly Pear, which I have heard of, and am excited to see. He says it is too far to walk, but it is a beautiful October day and I want to see the city, so off I go, on foot.

As I approach the Grisly Pear I walk by The Cellar and later learn I walked by the site of the Gaslight Cafe where Ms. Maisel performs in the Amazon series (in modern times it rests beneath a cookie shop). In more starry-eyed viewing I recognize a quiet street behind The Cellar where a Seinfeld documentary shows his joke pages laid out.

I arrive at the Grisly Pear but don't have time to get up on stage. I stay to watch a couple of comics perform. One was so bad the next comic starts his set by telling him to quit. Brutal, I guess New York City tough love really is a thing.

After dealing with lodging stuff, I am off to my first (almost) professional show as an audience member. A 7 p.m. Gotham Comedy Club new talent showcase. The entrance to Gotham is very fancy, a carpeted, well lit hallway with a hostess stand at the end and foreboding double doors, giving the impression that perhaps Heaven is on the other side. The hostess is surly and asks if I have a reservation.

A wave of panic hits. Crap. Is the show sold out? Maybe new-talent night in Manhattan is a bigger deal than I had guessed. And thus begins a series of comparisons between the Denver and New York City comedy scenes.

In a panic, I nervously blurt out, no, but I'm an out-of-town comic. I won't dive into the secret handshake that follows, but she quickly turns on the charm, and pretty soon I am in the back row of the club. When I ask if I can order a drink, I receive an invitation from the manager to wander into the kitchen and find the back-of-the house bar.

I had no idea this was only the beginning of a very special night. I feel like I have arrived. I daydream the talent manager will tell me he heard buzz about my open mic set earlier. What a fool. But a happy fool! That's the thing about comics in my experience, to have absurd levels of confidence, at least in spurts, is a requirement.

A new-talent night is an important part of any comedy scene. It allows developing comics to practice on a "real" stage with a "real" audience. I am so lucky to live in a city that has one. And a great one at that.

If open mics are where the soul goes to die, where material is sharpened to dangerous levels, the better to cut through the din of drunk and disinterested patrons, then "real" stage time is something entirely different. When done well, the butter is very hot. A limp noodle can cut it. A funny facial expression can produce a wave of laughs.

In Denver, New Talent Night is a marvel. Deacon Gray established a system that works wonderfully for comics and audience members. My Gotham experience makes me appreciate his influence on the program and the community that surrounds it. The Denver shows are packed. The laughs are hot and heavy. I can't think of a higher compliment.

The Gotham show is quite different. I'll just say it, perhaps with a touch of homerism. The newbies at Gotham are not very good. A win for Denver! In their defense, they were probably first timers, and they were doing five minutes. In Denver, your first time you get two minutes. Then you wait three months before you get three. Then it can be years, performing roughly once a quarter before you get four. Five minutes in Denver is reserved for touring comics, not rookies.

And frankly, the room was difficult on this night. It was at best forty percent full. And there are long lulls of boredom. Which, not to give anything away, makes what is about to happen all the more impressive. This dead fish room is about to get hot as a pocket.

There is no cost to perform at New Talent Night in Denver. I should mention here that open mics in Denver are free too, but it is common in New York City to pay five dollars to do five minutes. In a lesson I re-learn over and over, most painfully at my hotel, everything in New York City is more expensive.

The Gotham event is what is called a bringer show. That means each participant has to bring ten people (that number will vary by the show) who pay for a ticket and the drink minimum. So in a roundabout way, the comics are paying for their stage time by calling in favors from their friends' wallets. In Denver, every comic gets an unlimited number of free show tickets for friends, but those friends do need to cover a two-drink minimum. But you don't need to bring any friends.

I'll say one last point in favor of Denver. There is an incredible sense of community in Denver. Maybe not a fair comparison. I'm pretty sure after fifty open mics I know about two-thirds of every active Denver comic, it's just smaller. Pre-show at New Talent Night in Denver is a community gathering. Comics share jokes and tips. This is the office break room, and you see potluck style treats sometimes. During the show, comics hang out in the back row or a green room area. Clumps of them. In New York City, best I could see, the comics come alone and leave alone, like ships passing in the night. For the majority of this show, the only person with me in the back row was talent manager Andy Engel. Occasionally the host came by, a single comic, or the club manager.

At this point I don't have any more New Talent Night points for Denver, everything else is better in New York City. Starting with the host of New Talent night who was a serious comic with Comedy Central credits and national touring credits. The crowd is pretty weak but I can tell he is very good. In Denver's defense, there is a method to their hosting madness, as the hosts are learning the ropes for bigger and better things. The club uses the opportunity of hosting New Talent Night to develop homegrown talent so they can perform at shows that do not have readily accessible free tickets.

Denver mixes amateur and professional comedians to make for an entertaining new talent night, which is fun for the audience. The pros are not nationally recognizable household names, but they do make a living at comedy. New York City, at least on this night at Gotham Comedy Club is about to school Denver in this regard.

I am nursing my drink about five comics in when things get weird. I look up and standing right next to me is Mr. Hot Pockets himself, Mr. Jim Gaffigan. I can't believe it. Some people naturally play it cool around famous people. Not me. IT IS HIM. I CAN'T BELIEVE THIS IS HAPPENING. I pull it together and continue nursing my drink while he stands two feet from me. Should I laugh at the terrible jokes happening on stage? Should I play it cool and distant? I DON'T KNOW.

To make a long story short, the next lady up gets bumped for Jim to do twenty minutes of material he is working out. And this isn't like when I work material out, at one point I spit out part of my drink. He is FUNNY. And remember the dead room I mentioned? It is electric now. Stovetop hot. Would this turn around the entire night for other comedians? Not really. The next comic bombs HARD, it turns out.

When Jim is done he comes back, hangs out with me and the talent manager for ten minutes, says goodbye and goes. Everything nice you have ever heard about him is true.

I leave shortly after. But Gotham had one last NYC moment for me. Outside the talent manager is talking to someone, while I can't figure out which direction to start my Google Maps directions. Earlier inside we had spoken briefly. I had asked if I came back to NYC if I could get up on stage. He politely said no, not unless you bring ten people. He explained you can get up without bringing ten people but your last name needs to be Gaffigan or Seinfeld.

I ask for help and he politely tells me which way I want to walk and I say goodbye. As I head towards the subway he asks me how long I've been doing stand-up. Is this my big break? Before I even get "less than a year" out of my mouth, he lets out an exasperated sound of disappointment and disdain and completely turns his back to me. Welcome to New York kid.

My next stop is a late show at the Cellar. Which turns out to be an embarrassment of comedic riches.

I am seated center stage at a table, packed in. This is my first time at a venue I have seen on TV many times. It is a well oiled machine, ripe for the hot stove electricity that can bring laughs long and strong. Low ceilings, tight seating. Fire risk high. In comedy logic, the number of laughs will be too.

Tonight the host is Ian Fidance. He welcomes the opener Andrew Schulz to the stage. I have never heard of him, but I will not soon forget him. He starts out awkward. Almost daring you to find him funny. But he finishes so strong I become enamored with his style of punchy storytelling. The way he makes you hate him then wins you back. I later find out that even though I saw him just hanging out on the corner before the show, he is a character on Amazon's Sneaky Pete, and regularly sells out big venues as a headliner. He has well known podcasts, a million+ YouTube following and more. He is famous for having a comedy album that hit #1 with only self-promotion. He is a new kind of comic who abandoned the machine and created his own. I see him one more time in my three days in New York City because. Because NYC is an embarrassment of comedic riches.

Next are sets by Maria Franklin (Conan), Joe List (Netflix) and Dave Attell (many movie credits including Insomniac). Wow!

Then, with a stern reminder about the no-cell-phone policy, and to wild raucous cheers, they welcome a surprise (at least to me) drop-in appearance from Louis C.K. I don't know how he is as a co-worker, if he is a monster behind closed doors, but I can tell you what he is on stage: a phenom. He could go for three minutes about something as dumb as a styrofoam cup, and have me peeing my pants. Just an amazing talent. And I would see him twice more in the next twenty-four hours, which was an amazing workshop in observing comedy talent. I will see him do the same material multiple times, with small tweaks, but mostly, word for word, guttural sound for umm and uh exactly the same, best as I can tell. So well constructed. So well delivered. That even when I heard the same punchline a third time, I laugh. Hard.

Godfrey closes out the night, which is a special treat. When I was first starting he was someone I studied. In an ironic twist, he does a bit about how people don't go to the ballet and assume they can get up on stage and dance, but many folks think they can be a stand-up comedian. He says this notion is ridiculous. I know how right he is now, at this point in time, about me. Will he still be right if I stick at this for years?

I have been in New York for less than twelve hours. I have seen Gaffigan, Schulz, Attell, Godfrey and Louis C.K. Later I will tell some NY-based comics this and they will practically fall asleep with boredom. I had no idea this wasn't unusual. But the rest of my trip would give me some idea.

New York City obviously doesn't only offer comedy. I see a matinee Broadway play called Lifespan of a Fact. It is terrific. Daniel Radcliffe of Harry Potter fame stars, along with Bobby Cannavale (Mr. Robot and many other credits). The set design and production are terrific. Do you remember seeing The Social Network movie and thinking you had just experienced something special? I feel the same way about this play, because of how it modernizes the play-going experience in a way I feel The Social Network modernized cinema. Michelle Herring, the Denver comedian has told me about TodayTix which is an app for discounted Broadway tickets, and it works great.

On Wednesday I have set plans to see Elon Altman at West Side Comedy Club, which I later learn has been on Crashing. Elon and I met in Atlanta at the Red Clay Comedy Festival. When I wake up I buy tickets to the late show at The Cellar for that night. That's when I notice a ticket for sale that was not there yesterday. A five dollar ticket for something called Amy Schumer Pop Up at 5 p.m. around the corner from the Cellar.

The Amy Schumer thing is in the back room of the Fat Black Pussycat lounge. Using what I learned the night before I arrive early for best seating and am rewarded with a couch spot by the stage. To say it is on the stage would not be much of an exaggeration, neither would saying the stage was smaller than your standard subcompact car.

So is this friends of Amy? Does she host? Do they have a cardboard cut out of her? Will she pop up out of a cake? No idea, until she comes out with no host, and just launches into an hour of material she is working out, looking like she just rolled out of bed, still in what could be pajamas. She interacts with the crowd twice. Once she asks someone to move a stool on stage for her. Then mid-set she mercilessly and hilariously mocks me. ME! I laugh and cheer. New York City delivers again!

At West Side Comedy Club the showcase is a little weak, but it has highlights. Notably the host, Amarie Castillo, who does a great job getting the meager (a dozen people?) crowd involved and excited. Elon Altman and

Joe Larson are highlights at a show with more performers than audience members if you count the band that plays between acts.

Which makes it all the more remarkable when Louis is introduced and does the same material as the day before with minor tweaks.

After the show, I hang out in the back with some comedians and talk with Amarie who offers to get me some stage time if I'm staying in town. Are you kidding me? Heck yeah! Over the course of the next twelve hours, I get confirmed to do a showcase in Queens the next night.

Returning to the Cellar I see Andrew Schulz outside again, Louis is inside performing, and Godfrey closes out the late show, my eyes remain wide with excitement.

After another Broadway show (American Son with the star of Scandal, Kerry Washington), it is off to Woodside in Queens for a showcase at The Hive, where I do 5 minutes in front of a paid audience. I still can't believe it. If you ever read this Amarie, thank you.

In New York City everything is bigger. But is it really better? I'll be back again to see. I love comedy tourism.

Here is a bonus tip courtesy of Aaron Maslow, who once told me to start a spreadsheet and write down every out-of-town comedian you ever meet, so when you visit that town you can reach out. This has been very valuable advice and I encourage you to take it. If you want me to add you to my list, please contact me and let me know where you live. If I come through your town or city on comedy tourism, I would love to meet up.

Comedy-Mecca Visit - New York City

Comedy-Mecca Visit - Los Angeles

I spend 48 hours in Los Angeles to give a talk at a small conference and end up making a pretty good comedy experience out of it, even though I could have been more dedicated. The vastness of the city wears down on me and the stress of the speaking commitment definitely saps some energy.

If it was a success, the secret was a partner in crime ... with a car! An old Denver roommate and friend relocated to Oakland, and now a successful wedding photographer (mjoyphoto.com), drives down to hang out for a couple of days.

Turns out having a car is the most important thing you can have in Los Angeles. The place is huge! When I landed at LAX, I take a cab directly to the Melody Bar & Lounge which is across the street from the In N' Out Burger that is right next to the airport.

Folks are watching daytime NFL football in the bar, but in a side room, there are about a dozen comedians doing time and providing each other feedback. I bring my luggage in, grab a booth, watch two comedians, and then am on stage for five minutes. Per usual I set up my recording equipment, a small video camera and phone in the back of the room. The mic is a terrific experience.

I do my best material at the time, which is mostly Airbnb stuff and it gets a warm reaction. This mic is a little like a workshop, and people provide feedback. After my set, we get into a discussion about the merits and disadvantages of my clean comedy when someone encourages me to swear and several people say I should stay clean.

Once the mic breaks up, I do my usual thing, I say hi to some comedians, tell them I am from out of town and am looking for other mics. You can find information online but sometimes it is wrong, and real in-person conversations tend to yield the best results for me.

By asking locals you can find out how long sets are, if mics have decent crowds, and other details that are usually not online. In a town where I would find out they have open mics in the back of trucks in a parking lot, this was exactly the right time and place to ask questions in person.

The first person I talk to is a comedian transplant from San Francisco, Ben Horowitz, who runs an open mic at the Ha Ha Cafe in Hollywood, that happens to be tonight. Perfect!

I check into a mediocre hotel in Santa Monica and get some dinner, and then it is off to more comedy. In a classic comedy misfire, we go to Westside Comedy Club for a mic. Westside is a small theater I remember from seeing George Wallace work out material once at a showcase, but tonight turns out to be much less special.

The mic has been canceled and the alley is full of annoyed comics.

We head to Hollywood, and after some great drinks at a Mexican restaurant end up at Ha Ha Cafe. I'll discuss this more in depth in another chapter, but let's just say this was a unique experience for me in a couple of ways. It costs money, five dollars for five minutes or ten dollars for ten minutes. It is a bucket show, with a next-up announcement, so you have some prep time, but the order is random. I manage to film my set as a timelapse video by accident, and later spend an hour matching up phone audio with the time-lapse video, making what was already just an OK performance look like some awful stop-motion cinema art.

After my time, I stick around for a few more comedians and then we head over to the Laugh Factory. The Laugh Factory holds a special place in my heart because a long time ago I saw a younger Tiffany Haddish do stand-up there. Her jokes that night mostly surrounded how famous she was going to become because of a movie (Girls Trip, it turns out) that had just been shot. The small audience was not sure what to think, but after the show, she was super nice and took pictures with me and a friend. Later when I realized her prediction had come true, I think a kernel was planted in my head that magic happens behind a microphone, and that was just one of many seeds that eventually led to my first-ever open-mic performance.

On this night there was different star power on hand and a packed house. Dane Cook is working out new material but we miss him. Jamie Masada, the owner of the Laugh Factory, is hanging in the room at the front of the club. He graciously allows us to watch from the balcony area, which we have to ourselves, and it is a terrific show.

Seeing professional comedians do their thing is a brutal reminder of how far I have to go. I know funny after thousands of open mic performances, and usually, it comes in dribs and drabs, but some of these comedians have me roaring for ten or twenty minutes straight. Amazing.

The rest of the weekend doesn't involve much more comedy although we catch one more pro show at the Magic and Comedy Club, where Jay Leno headlines every Monday night. It is less interesting than the Laugh Factory show but still a unique performance, and Mr. Leno is impressive in the length of his sets and is an absolute comedy legend.

When I go back to Los Angeles I will hit some other live shows at places like the Largo Theater, and look for smaller showcases, and definitely hit more mics. I'll plan on a longer trip and be sure to have a car. Do you have any comedy tourism tips for my next visit to the city of angels? Please share!

Young Comics Steal Jokes

Mimicking other comedians is how I started in comedy. Maybe some geniuses are originals from the start, but that wasn't me when I was just learning to crawl as a comedian. Imitation can be nuanced and there are different levels of what can be described as pattern matching, ranging from the innocent to the vile. There are at least fifty shades of joke thievery, is what I'm saying.

These are my thoughts at six months, based on my observations and feelings. This can be a polarizing topic and you may have your own feelings and ideas. Feel free to reach out and discuss if you agree or your perspective differs.

I'll structure this naive discussion of joke stealing by categorizing the types of theft. Keep in mind some of these topics are definitely not a bad kind of joke stealing. There is a spectrum from acceptable to unacceptable.

The categories I'll cover are blatant borrowing (completely unacceptable), disconnected discovery (completely innocent), premise poaching and word wrangling.

Let's start at a place everyone can agree on, that blatant joke stealing, word for word, literal copying is repulsive. There are YouTube videos where foreign language comics lift entire routines from well known American comedians. Some have even led to lawsuits.

At the open mic level this kind of blatant burglary manifests itself on occasion. Sometimes, an open mic first timer will lift an entire bit from a well known comedian or read jokes off a print out from the internet. I have seen both of these happen and never saw the performers again. I call this kind of very bad joke stealing **blatant borrowing**.

Blatant borrowing is the most obvious form of joke theft and the worst. It is easy to spot and to confirm. Other categories of joke stealing can be more subjective and not necessarily even bad. They can take some practice to spot and understand.

With six months of comedy under my belt, I now appreciate more subtlety than I would have predicted, when I went to my first open mic.

To dive deeper into joke stealing, specifically an innocent form, let me exercise a misdirect, with a joke of mine and a question.

I am an Airbnb host, which makes me different from other up-and-coming comedians.
Tonight my place is rented, so right now ... I am making money

I can't wait to celebrate this later ...
While sleeping in my car

This is a solid bit from my first half-year of comedy. It is personal, it has two punchlines in quick succession, and it is self-deprecating. People sometimes wonder if sleeping in my car is an exaggeration, as a lot of humor is, or is it a form of truth?

The short answer is the truth.

The long answer will meander into joke stealing territory in an unexpected way. It is a story of one of my most frustrating experiences as a newer comic and joke writer, during my first six months.

I have a small Airbnb property a long drive from where I live, and I needed it cleaned on two successive nights, and could not find a cleaner. I have day tripped to do a single clean before, but this was a new situation for me, I didn't want to day trip on consecutive days.

I decided I could "car camp" between cleans, which is a generous way to describe sleeping in the back of my Subaru Outback. To soften the blow I planned a nice bike ride and trail run, which basically made this the most Colorado adventure ever.

After completing my first clean I had some extra time before guest arrival and was in no hurry to get out there and "camp". I watched a comedy documentary on Netflix about Jerry Seinfeld. It had a story arc about Orny Adams. I had never heard of Mr. Adams so I downloaded his comedy albums for future listening.

I regularly do this, I'll hear tell of a comedian I was previously unfamiliar with and listen to all of their albums. It is fun! And it is a great learning opportunity. (I am a Google Play Music subscriber, and comedy albums are included with music albums, check your streaming service for similar.)

As night fell I drove my car to a dark corner of town where I hoped I would not be bothered by the police. I set up a memory foam mattress in the back of my wagon and laid down a sleeping bag.

I slept, kind of. It was a very cold Colorado night. While getting ready I had brushed my teeth and spit in the dirt and reflected that if I am ever good enough as a comedian to do road work, this could be my future. It didn't feel very glamorous, but at the same time, weirdly, it sounded desirable. I had a vision of a slightly nicer experience, perhaps owning a Tesla, which could quietly run, and heat or cool, while I slept in the back.

At dawn I was awake, and fearing discovery, got a move on. I went to a public transportation center in town to clean up and wait for a coffee shop to open, where I could work on my writing.

In the bathroom, after brushing my teeth, I was alarmed to not find a paper towel to dry my toothbrush, before putting it back in my backpack. Instead, there was only the ominously named Dyson Airblade, which comically expected me to put my hands inside it. With tremors from a poor night's sleep, I bumped the edges of the Airblade and immediately thought this was like a game of Operation, that I was not winning. In the most disgusting fashion. This is comedy, I thought!

I found a bench and table in the transportation center and wrote out an entire bit about the bathroom experience, longhand. I was very proud of it.

Later in the day while doing the second clean I listened to the Orny Adams albums distractedly. At one point he discusses a bathroom in a fancy restaurant. The topic caused me to listen a little more closely.

When he mentioned the lack of paper towels, I stopped what I was doing.

When he mentioned an air machine I sat down.

I made an oath to unleash a mighty F-bomb if he mentioned the game Operation.

Moments later, I released a mighty F-bomb, I was furious!

The timing was remarkable. Some words were, of course, different, but the kernel of what was funny, the premise, and even some of the punchlines were remarkably similar. How was this possible? Did Orny Adams time travel and steal my material?!

Of course not. As I would learn over time, many comedians independently discover material that is basically the same. Some people refer to this as parallel thinking. But I like alliterations, so I am calling it **disconnected discovery**, which I think is more descriptive anyway.

Realizing you have been the victim of disconnected discovery sucks. I can't tell you what a pit in the stomach feeling it is to see someone on stage start a bit that you have previously written. And occasionally a feeling of triumph when you realize your best punchline has yet to be discovered in your overlapping premises.

This terrible feeling is what drives me to write more original and unique material as I progress, but it is hard when you struggle to make the low-hanging fruit funny, to reach that good stuff.

Some say a skilled comedian is able to choose material so personal and unique that it cannot be stolen. But by virtue of some comedy being relatable, this can't always be the case. Even Gary Gulman tells jokes about going to Chipotle, after all.

I recall being at Syntax Physic Opera, an open mic bar in Denver, when an out-of-town comedian from Canada did a bit about how racist it was that the scary Spice Girl was black. A local comedian, Wes Williams, had been doing that same joke for weeks, and in fact, went on stage about an hour later and did it again. I don't think anyone thought of it as stealing. Just a coincidence.

Just, disconnected discovery.

I saw Jim Gaffigan do some horse-related jokes in New York City, and then about a month later an accomplished, very original and funny local comedian (Jacob Rupp) was doing a series of horse jokes also. I felt bad that soon he might see a Jim Gaffigan special and realize his jokes had been burned. Perhaps, since in this case, it was the topic and not the exact jokes, maybe he could continue telling them.

But again, disconnected discovery.

If there were a comedy court, maybe it would matter who first originated an idea, but in practice, this common phenomenon is more likely to be responded to with shrugs than accusations. It can be frustrating, but generally, you just abandon your joke and move on, once you realize your idea is not as original as maybe you hoped.

Here are some personal examples of disconnected discovery I experienced in my first six months.

I did a joke about a hipster not getting that there was media before podcasts, he proudly tells a friend about PBS which he thinks is an innovative network called P as in Podcast, BS, with tons of content, and a revolutionary delivery technique that pairs videos and photos with the standard podcast audio. About a week later a local comedian told a joke on stage about his super (maintenance man) confusing podcasts and AM radio. I don't know if I inspired him or he was making sure I knew he had a similar joke, too, or if we came up with the same rough idea in the same timeframe. I've learned over time it doesn't really matter. The better you get at writing jokes, the less you care about burned material. I also always try to assume good intent.

Another example. I was driving home from the airport after a red-eye (this is the 1 a.m. flight following an awful open mic night in San Francisco) and turned on NPR. It was around 5 a.m. so they were playing BBC news segments. There was word of a horrible bombing, which gave me a surge of adrenaline until I realized they were not talking about something that happened in America. It was a disgusting reaction, but I had it, and so I wrote a joke about it where the repeated punchline was "in Afghanistan". Shortly after another Denver comic did a joke at Mutiny Cafe, about people dying in Chicago, but not being alarmed once she learned they were "old people".

In both these cases, it is possible that the timing meant they were politely letting me know they had found the material "first". I don't think either topic is remarkably original, and they were more veteran than I was at comedy. So it makes sense that I would be the later comic to write similar material.

I say this because now I can appreciate being on the other side.

It took a while before this pattern happened in the opposite direction, meaning someone told a joke stepping on my material, months after I had told it. Finally, I was the "veteran". When it did, my immediate reaction was a sudden urge to tell my similar joke when I got on stage, or the next time I saw that comedian.

Let's switch gears to **premise poaching**, which is a little higher on the vile scale but when you are just getting started can be hard to avoid. New comedians are a bit like chameleons, they hear something funny and ape it. Could be from a Netflix special, a comedy album, or in person at a mic. Could be mannerisms, speaking style, or topics. If you are new, I want to emphasize that I don't see anything terribly wrong with behaving like a chameleon in small doses, you should be experimenting, trying everything you can to see what works for you. Just don't let copying become a habit.

The word premise can be fuzzy so when we talk about premise poaching I want to use a broad definition, which I'll explain by example.

If we look at a series of words:

Football, NFL Football, NFL Football referees, NFL Football referees are blind

You can see they increase in specificity. With any borrowing, the more specific the idea you are borrowing, the worse.

If someone tells a joke about NFL referees being blind and needing canes, and you write a joke about NFL referees being blind because their contacts fell out, you have poached a premise.

If you hear the cane joke and then tell a joke about playground football, you can say you were inspired by someone else's joke but it is less offensive. If the idea of football as a sport inspires you to write a hockey joke, that is even more innocent.

As you grow as a comedian, you should try to only do what you consider original work, but I'll assert that when you are starting, some borrowing is going to happen and as long as you don't get into a habit of it, and intend to grow out of it, it is ok.

Premise poaching is not quite as innocent as disconnected discovery, but the two sometimes can be confused, especially from an outsider's perspective.

One day nobody has a Bandersnatch joke, one week after the Netflix show comes out, ten comedians tell a Bandersnatch joke. Do some of them have the same take on Bandersnatch and what makes it funny? That's where we might have trouble.

Is the prevalence because the first comedian did a joke and it spread, or because the topic became part of the zeitgeist? Who knows. Often only the comedian telling a joke will ever know the origin of their material.

The more obscure the topic, the more likely it is premise poaching.

This is such a common phenomenon that even I have thought my premises may have been poached. I have even had other comedians alert me to it.

Did I confront the potential poachers? No. The general attitude towards confrontation on these issues I see, is that none of us are recording specials, so who really cares unless there is a very consistent pattern. Which I'm happy to report I have yet to see in Denver.

Premise poaching is a mild version of joke stealing common with amateurs that are not experienced. They hear a topic and think "that is funny", and they see another comedian making it funny, so they figure if they do their own take on it, maybe it will be funny too.

I think if you are not stealing punchlines, then go ahead in the very early days. Just realize people will probably notice and you should get better and knock it off as quickly as you can. I also would not tell those jokes on a show, should you be lucky enough to get on one. At open mics, well, the bar is more flexible for what is wrong. Everyone is figuring something out.

It is kind of fun actually when you go to open mics five nights a week to watch, like a C.D.C. epidemiologist, the spread of an idea, from experienced funny comedian to less funny newbies.

I was the first person in my local scene to tell an Airbnb joke I am pretty sure. I have entire routines about Airbnb. I have since seen at least one amateur and one professional in my local scene telling Airbnb jokes. Should I care? No. I don't own Airbnb humor, so how could I be upset? Good for them noticing (if they did, maybe it was disconnected) a funny topic to mine for humor and getting something from my participation in the scene.

Remember that other premises are everywhere. Always have your comedian brain on and be listening for funny stories, or things to write jokes about, and write them down right away. This can help you avoid premise poaching. And live life! Go experience new things. The funny will find you if you get out there.

Word wrangling is the little brother to premise poaching. Instead of taking a premise topic, you just take a funny word to punch up or tag something you have. Again, impossible to say who thought it first, but you can have a suspicion. Also impossible to say how intentional it is. The weirder the word(s), the more likely it is to be some form of intentional. Kumquat. Kangaroo pouch. You get the idea.

I suspect weak comics feel like if they get the right word into a joke with no punchline, it will be funnier. Spoiler alert, it usually isn't.

I have seen enough attempts like this, probably some of my own even (which I'd like to forget) to confirm this suspicion.

It would be outlandish for me to say I have never been close to the joke-stealing line. As a very new comedian, my tools were so rough, the best I could often do was mimic the motions of others, like a child learning to walk. I am certain I borrowed funny words and premises because writing is a muscle and mine was weak.

I was trying to figure out how to stand on stage without passing out, and how to adjust a mic stand, so the origin of my jokes seemed unimportant at the time, but now, I'm embarrassed to admit it.

Hindsight being 20/20, the signs are clear. Here is one example where I was more thief than muse-inspired writer.

Dave's Killer Bread.

Just those three words.

I saw a very funny local comedian do a bit about it, and within a week I had a not very good joke that had the same three words. Not the same punchline, but the same topic. You can call it premise poaching or word wrangling, but either way, I call it not my best look. I told the joke a couple of times, and now it sits abandoned in one of my notebooks, just another failed attempt. It never did well. Serves me right.

I am resolved now to talk to that comedian and apologize. I have a suspicion he will have a forgiving attitude.

The topic was the same but the jokes were different. I was a brand-new comedian. It wasn't like I was recording an album or anything. It didn't impact him at all. If I never got better at joke writing and didn't learn to create my own content, I would quit. Probably he'll say those kinds of things.

Actually, more likely he will say … who are you again?

Here is another story, about a professional, that I saw at the Laugh Factory in Hollywood, California. I think this story speaks to the complexity and nuance of joke thievery.

This very accomplished nationally touring comedian did a joke that had "minty" in the punchline that I knew I had heard before. It took me a few weeks to track it down, but when I found it I almost couldn't believe how similar it was. The setup was slightly different but the punchline was word for word the same. It was from (the deceased) Garry Shandling's 1981 appearance on Johnny Carson which you can find online and is amazing. It has so many jokes per minute it is astonishing.

Who stole the "minty" punchline? I have no idea. And perhaps the answer is nobody.

It is entirely possible one of the comedians sold the other their joke or gave it, or independently found it, and discussed that they both could use it. Or it is possible they both stole it from an old vaudeville routine. I have no idea, but experiencing that, I felt a little better about my Dyson Airblade game-of-Operation joke, which I burned before ever performing. To my utter despair at the time.

I have other jokes where a similar word, like a homonym, is part of a joke I will later hear another comedian tell. Overlap is not theft, is my attitude, today. Maybe when I get even better I'll take a harder line and it will be so easy to generate good content I'll regularly abandon bits. For now, if a joke isn't doing well anyways, an overlap discovery can earn it an early grave, but if I know in my heart I wrote a joke independently and I'm proud of it, I will keep telling it.

I'll tell one last story that will speak to how what can look like joke stealing is often not joke stealing.

I was in a green room once with a nationally touring comedian. A very funny national news story had occurred that day and several comedians were discussing it. The headliner mentioned he had started writing jokes about it already. Hours later at an open mic, I saw another comedian kill with jokes covering the same premise. Nobody stole from anybody. Some premises are just open to everyone ... and so ripe for humor.

Said another way, funny is universal. Which increases the possibility of you and someone else thinking the same exact thing is funny, independently.

Which can drive you a little crazy before you realize if you work really hard at writing, your comedy muscle will improve and you can write practically unlimited new funny stuff.

When my muscle was weak I wrote a joke about Jeff Bezos (specifically his right eye) looking like Sloth from Goonies. It felt so obvious I had to turn to the internet. I was relieved after Googling it, that there appeared to be nobody else using it. Then, of course, I became concerned it might not be funny. Man, you can never win as a comedian!

If you are still in your first one hundred mic's, I wouldn't sweat this topic too much if you aren't literally stealing word for word. Be aware of joke stealing and try to minimize it. Know you'll probably do it, even accidentally, and as long as you are new, no one will judge you too harshly.

But it is worth talking about. One of my favorite conversation starters with more experienced comedians has become, "have you ever had a joke stolen?"

Try it sometime. I find it yields a quality exploration into the history and experience of the comedian you are conversing with. It's also fun to hear them share old jokes, that usually they never tell anymore.

As for yourself, and your comedy writing, hopefully, you will soon be a good enough comedy writer to avoid any form of stealing.

Or you will quit.

My Shows And Gigs As A Performer

You may or may not have gigs in your first six months. I was lucky enough to have a few. Most came about by accident and occurred when I was ill prepared for them. I found time and again that saying Yes, and setting myself up for achievement drove me to work even harder. Yes, it meant some failures along the way, but comedy is about failing. Embrace it, and you will come out the other side better for it if you put in the work.

Keep in mind I never asked to be on a local show. I still haven't. Don't go bothering local people to get on their shows. They have the opportunity to discover you, and will if you are ready. That's the message I heard early on and have stuck to.

But if an opportunity does land in your lap, even if it is terrifying, say Yes! This is a lesson I learned from a great Chicago (by way of Denver) comedian Pat Treuer. This sentiment also echoes a story that Mike Birbiglia tells about the first time he is asked if he can do thirty minutes.

No matter how I ended up on a show, I am glad for all of them. I learned important lessons, and I got practical experience. Reading books and listening to podcasts is fun, but you really don't improve unless you are out there with real audiences.

My Shows And Gigs As A Performer

My first show ever was an open-air show at the Skyline Park Beer Garden in Downtown Denver. Right underneath the famous 16th St. Mall Clocktower building. I got on the show by accident. I went to a now defunct, mostly black, contest open mic hosted by Dick Black at The Living Room. I did OK but didn't win the contest, Anthony Armstrong, a terrific local comedian did.

But I did run into a very drunk comedian who told me he was putting a show on and he wanted me on it. To this day I think he confused me with someone else. I got his phone number and followed up a few days later. Sure enough, he had time for me if I could show up, and would even pay me two dollars a minute.

I ended up doing seventeen minutes including a very long meandering story I wrote that day as a time filler. When I realized I hadn't got a photograph (my first paying gig!) I actually went back up for a few more minutes so I could get a picture taken. I wasn't ready for this amount of time or crowd but I got laughs, and people noticed me, and it was a real thrill and confidence booster for me. I will never forget it.

This gig also motivated me to put together a basic website. The pressure of an event to do that was a great kick in the pants. My point is sometimes stage time can push you to do other things, maybe get a quality headshot, set up a Twitter account, etc.

The next time I went up at a show was in Pueblo, CO. I was driving to Santa Fe, New Mexico for a wedding, and was trying to find stage time. I was looking for an open mic along the way, but I found a comedy show instead. The location was great to break up my drive. When I got there, early, I introduced myself and they asked me if I would do time. When they found out I was from Denver they bumped me up to a feature (the spot just before the headliner). I didn't deserve any of this.

But again I was in the right place at the right time and got lucky. What's that saying, most of life is showing up? Combine that with saying Yes and you have my recipe for getting opportunities.

But what a disaster! This was at a rough bar in a rough part of town, and although there was an audience of about thirty people, which was big for me, only about four people were listening. The others were fighting, yelling, even motorboating each other (during my set, what a distraction!).

I had five minutes of Airbnb material to go through and I started by asking if anyone knew what Airbnb was. When legitimately nobody in the bar could say they had, I knew I was in big trouble, but I had nothing else to do but power through my memorized material. It was bad, very bad.

But what a motivator to figure out how to engage a crowd better in the future. I definitely needed more road jokes (quick, dirty, hacky) and an ability to do crowd work. I needed questions I could work into punchy quips. I'm glad I did this show and will be back when I am a better comedian.

I didn't bump anyone more experienced and was helping a showrunner fill time. The show led me to submit a piece of comedy writing that eventually was published in a book. I would definitely have done it the same way again if I had to. I left with audio and video recordings that I was able to study and use to make improvements.

My next show was in Westminster, Colorado, a suburb between Denver and Boulder. I had been on a professional panel and another panel member had a business that needed entertainment at a holiday party. It came up that I was into comedy and I gave her a business card. Her assistant ended up contacting me and booking me for a fifteen-minute show for fifty dollars. Fifty dollars!

I learned a great deal about recording at this gig. I set up two different video cameras and had a two-channel audio recording made with a Zoom H4N. One channel was the audience and the other was the feed from the mic which ran into a speaker system I brought and set up.

This show went pretty well. It started late which messed with my schedule and made it even less profitable, but I did have about fifteen minutes of mediocre material at what was about five months in. I even got paid!

My last show was in Queens, NY and was in the middle of a legitimate showcase I had no business being on. Again I think it was a miscommunication, who knows. I had gone to a comedy show in Manhattan on the upper west side, and during the hostess's crowd work, it came out that I was trying comedy. After the show, I met her and I think she got the impression that I had been at a comedy festival with another performer on that show.

This was kind of true, but I was a volunteer and audience member at the comedy festival, not a performer.

Either way, I did end up in a showcase at an antique shop with performance space in Woodside, a neighborhood in Queens, NY. Subway transportation was relatively easy and the place was very cute. I got a free drink and a very long wait for the show which started over an hour after it was supposed to.

I did about as well as you might have expected. The show included touring comedians, and I was not very good in comparison. In fact, my opening joke was terrible, just a total miss. Always lead with a really good, well practiced first joke. I wrote something that day which was a bonehead move.

I'm glad I did the show though, and I learned a lot. My biggest regret was leaving the show early. I had skipped dinner to get there early and it was so late I felt I had to. As it was, several restaurants ended up being closed as a result of the late hour.

None of my show stories are very crazy, but if I have learned anything worth re-emphasizing, it is you have to be out there for great things to happen. Let people know you do comedy even in non-comedy settings. Attend a lot of comedy events, go to every open mic you can. You never know when magic is going to strike and lead to a stage appearance.

Say Yes to everything.

And then put in the work to deliver to the best of your ability.

Can You Learn Comedy?

This six-month experiment is fun, but it is also an intellectual challenge to myself. Can someone become funny by studying funny? Is funny a teachable topic? In my experience it is, and it is deceptively complex.

When I was in college I taught myself a programming technique, recursion, that until Organic Chemistry was the hardest thing I had ever learned, and I was so proud to have understood it by applying myself. Unexpectedly, comedy has eclipsed all these prior studies as the most difficult thing I have attempted as a student.

Who knew there was so much technical skill involved in this craft? And so much writing!

I never before thought about how clarity, compression, and contrast could be used to make other people laugh. I'm not even sure I knew those words in the context of comedy. (Hat tip to Harrison Greenbaum for the triplet of C's, I also love his "new, true and you" joke maxim)

I never before came up with a premise and evaluated how to make it funny on stage. I never ran stage experiments on what combination of exaggeration, understatement, misdirection, unspoken conclusion, or act-out would generate the most consistent and reliable audience laughter.

I never watched a set and evaluated what kind of humor the comedian was using. But now I can identify many types: observational, anecdotal, put down, self-deprecation, speaking the unspeakable, character act, and specialty (like magic and props).

I also never thought I would know a word like paraprosdokian, or come to discover that I use paraprosdokians regularly.

Someone once said that comedy is lying and poetry put together, which doesn't seem like something you could study. E.B. White famously said that "Analyzing humor is like dissecting a frog. Few people are interested and the frog dies of it."

But I'll assert after 6 months, this idea is wrong.

You can study comedy. You can study people who are funny. You can study why things make people laugh, and you can improve your ability to create things that make people laugh with this study and practice. You can iterate ideas through experimentation by telling varied versions of jokes to audiences, in fact, this turns out to be what even professional comedians do until they find just the right cadence and combination of words that yields the most laughs.

I have learned that there are patterns to the surprise and delight that confuse an audience member's brain into causing unexpected laughter.

I am still not good at reliably creating content that makes people laugh, but I improve every week, with more practice and study. I improve by consuming content about comedy. And I improve by watching comedy, from open mic comedians all the way up to professionals. This study has led to jokes I originated, being told on stage by me, resulting in audience laughter. What a thrill and a fun positive-feedback loop.

We live in an incredible age of information. I encourage all beginning comics in a local scene to find a podcast by a local comedian. If you are as lucky as I was with Talkin' Shop by Anthony Crawford, you can consume years of material in weeks, and get up to speed on your scene like Neo in the Matrix learning to fly a helicopter, faster than should be possible.

You can watch the Stand-Up mastery talk by Ralphie May online for free. An hour and forty-five minutes from one of the greats.

You can spend almost four hours watching video of Ari Shaffir break down stand-up comedy for students.

You can read books and listen to podcasts and watch live comedy and become a lifelong student of what is funny.

Aristotle suggested in Rhetoric that a good joke relies on setting an expectation and then violating it. Aristotle! People have been studying comedy forever.

Can You Learn Comedy?

Can you learn how to be a comedian, how to be funny, enough so to be a successful comedian? I can't tell you that yet for sure, but I encourage you to check back with me. At the moment all signs point to yes. I am already much better, but certainly far from good, at predicting what will be funny, at flexing my comedy writing muscle, and at making people laugh.

Might I plateau before I reach the level of a working professional comedian, paid to make people laugh? I guess it is possible, but at the tail end of six months, my improvement train shows no signs of slowing down.

There was a line in the HBO series Crashing where a character dismissively says "he'll be funny in three years." I think I understand that now. It takes time and practice and study to get reliably funny for audiences.

Even though I am better than six months ago, I still get surprised by audiences, where the rubber meets the road. But even that experience gives me confidence in how time spent honing this craft can lead to future success.

For example, I have a joke with a sports-team reference. I didn't guess what is obvious in hindsight, that when I told it, sometimes people would cheer in the audience when I mentioned the team's name. I spoke right over them accidentally the first time I did it in front of a large enough crowd.

With the benefit of this knowledge though, which I earned with practice, now when someone does make a loud noise, I can make a quip that sounds like a spur of the moment riff, but isn't. Then that gets an even bigger laugh, and it compounds the laughter for the still-to-come punchline such that it gets more laughs than it ever would have on its own.

This success appears to be part of a pattern, the result of a comedy nerd who has studied hard, and practiced hard, and is using his experience to deliver a better audience experience. I hope I can repeat it over and over again.

I am not trying to say that there is no spontaneity in comedy performances (see my story from my New York trip), but I do believe now that good comedy is the result of more practice than I had once assumed.

If you are reading this and thinking you could never be funny on stage, take solace in the fact that the comedians you have seen kill on stage probably worked on their material for years and practiced it hundreds of times before you heard it. If you are willing to practice hundreds of times and put in the same number of years they have, you can create the same illusion for an audience.

There are lots of amazing local comedians, who genuinely make me laugh out loud when I see their new material (Michael Isaacs and Anthony Crawford jump to mind). Later, when I see the same bit again, I realize it was the result of a great comedic mind and preparation, and the delivery gave it the appearance of being off the cuff, but it was actually practiced and prepared.

It is fun and motivating that just by watching and enjoying their material, I can be pushed to get better and work harder. Find the people in your own scene who motivate you.

Now I just need to spend my next six months determining if a good comedic mind can be grown with training and practice. Maybe I won't even get to good, but I think I will be better. When I reflect on any success I have had, and think of it in the context of my first open mic, I am amazed by how far I have come.

My opinion at this point in my comedy career is that you can science comedy. You can go from terrible to mediocre with the same tools that helped me learn recursion and Organic Chemistry. Especially if you practice patience and discipline.

Luckily, stand-up comedy is a lot more fun than those school subjects.

Christmas Letter

My family has one of those old-school Christmas letters where everyone writes an update for who knows what audience. Below is my contribution for 2018 with some sections removed to keep this about just me and comedy. Note that I had not shared my comedy pursuits with my family until this letter. This was written towards the end of my first six months.

[removed]

By a long shot, that was not the pursuit that presented this year's biggest challenge.

Adam Cayton-Holland once said in a set on Conan O'Brien "When you become a stand-up comedian, you tell your parents I think I wanna be a comic. And they're ashamed of you. And that's correct. And then you headline like one or two shows and your parents get to tell a few choice people. And then you get on TV once ... and they tell freaking everybody."

I'm far from ever being on TV, to be clear, but I did ask myself this year what might be an uncomfortably exciting hobby to pursue. When I found something that involved sleeping in, binge-watching TV, meeting famous people, reading, writing, and laughing a lot, I was hooked.

On top of [removed], I tried stand-up comedy. Seriously!

Christmas Letter

I watched, listened, and read about comedy obsessively this year. And after a couple of dry runs, on June 25th, I stood in front of strangers and tried to make them laugh. Predictably, it was excruciating, for me, and the audience.

About six months later, I write almost every day. I get up on stage multiple times a week. Sometimes I wait several hours just for a couple of minutes behind a microphone. After performing in six states, I can at least say this. I am improving. Every day I get better. And it remains uncomfortably exciting.

When I went to New York City this fall I was surprised to see Louis C.K. (who has sold out Madison Square Garden) three times in two days, once with twelve people in the audience. It was almost as surprising as hanging out with Jim Gaffigan while sitting in the back of a comedy club. Or being inches from Amy Schumer for an hour, and having her make a joke at my expense (I laughed).

I did a small showcase while in New York City, and to perform there, for a paying audience no less, was a thrill. More recently I went to Los Angeles. I got up on stage a few times and met the owner of the Laugh Factory. He graciously let me sit in the balcony for free, and watch real professionals show off their skill. It was the most hilarious and fun way to realize how far I have to go.

I started organizing comedy shows, which is how many unknown comedians get stage time. If you create the show, you can put yourself on it. I put on one show near Coors Field in Denver this December. Over one hundred people attended. I was the host and did more than five minutes of material I had worked on over many months, on many stages, to warm up the crowd for seven other comedians. I was more confident and relaxed, and unlike that first time, this was fun, for me and the audience.

As I was lugging stuff to my car afterward, an audience member pulled me aside and said, "I had a rough day at work today, and needed that, thanks for all the laughs."

I don't know how long I will stay at this, but it was something I never thought I could do. So I am glad I tried it. In [removed] your audience sometimes never provides feedback, but in comedy, for better or for worse, the feedback is always instantaneous. When it is good, as in laughter and applause breaks, it makes all the hours in crappy bars, all the time writing and rewriting, all the nerves and worry, more than 100% worth it.

Mom, Dad - Surprise. I think I wanna be a comic. Prepare to be ashamed. For a long time.

But someday, maybe you can tell freaking everyone. I imagine it will still be uncomfortably exciting.

Ed. note: My parents are truly the best, when they received this my Dad responded "Bravo. What made you think our love was conditional? Do what you like and compensation will follow. May the wind be at your

Christmas Letter

back..." They also sent the photo of a younger me that I hope makes the final printing of this book.

The Big Show: Holiday Ha Ha Ha

On December 4, 2018, I put on a show called Holiday Ha Ha Ha. It was a holiday party for a large local Meetup group called Denver Founders Network. Over one hundred people filled the chairs for the free show. It was held at the Soda Pop Garage two blocks away from Coors Field in Downtown Denver. Seven amazing comedians performed, in addition to the host, myself, Mark Masters.

It was a ton of work setting up the venue, marketing the event, organizing the talent, running the audio-visual components (including a hype video I produced as well as customized backdrops for each performer), and making sure professional audio and video recordings of the show were made without a hitch.

It was also the best thing I could have done, to inspire me to keep going for another six months.

I got to warm up the cold crowd, with seven minutes of material, some of it tailored to the mostly entrepreneurial crowd. It hit, and it hit hard. Folks were laughing out loud. At me! At jokes I had written! What a validation of all the hard work I had put in for the last six months.

A few hours later I would be at an open mic unable to get a hardened group of comedians to laugh, but for this bright and shining moment, all was right in my comedy journey.

The event wasn't perfect. I forgot to light one of the performers. Between a few acts, I went on too long and lost some crowd energy. The front row wasn't seated which made the video look less great than it should have. My audience-reaction camera lost battery during the performance. I made the cardinal sin of not making the last thing I said in my host introduction of a performer, their name. A couple of times.

But overall, it was a hit. It was a redemption, worthy of all my efforts. And not just the efforts explicitly for this event. I mean all my comedy efforts. The late nights in bars and coffee shops, the early mornings writing, the afternoons spent reading and studying, all of it came to a head in front of bright lights and a hundred seated audience members.

When I told my first joke about the time I did a set in Las Vegas, and it hit, I relaxed. Watching the video I can see myself loose and having fun on stage. I look like an athlete that knows they have put in the time. Confident they can do this.

Also, watching it now, months later, I experience the curse of any comedian. I cringe a little. Why did I tell *that* joke? I have much better material now!

How did this event happen? Like with so much in my first six months, I willed it to be.

For several years I have attended this particular holiday party. I knew the organizers usually paid for a DJ. I reached out over a month in advance and offered to provide entertainment this year for free, in the form of a comedy show.

Unbeknownst to me, they had recently turned over leadership and the new organizers were still figuring things out. As a result, they were thrilled with the offer to help. They agreed to take a chance on a comedy show. Luck favors the prepared, my friends!

I chose who would perform based on watching over a thousand stand-up sets from local comics over the last half of a year. I also factored in who had been thoughtful and helpful to me along the way.

When I invited the performers, I promised them a small cash payment from my own pocket, stage time in front of a large audience, promotion online, and a professional recording of their set. I was pleasantly surprised that anyone said yes, but they all did.

The performers in order of appearance were Austin Black, Sammy Anzer, Michael Isaacs, Nic Dean, Georgia Comstock, Alan Bromwell, and Zac Maas.

During the show, an audience member passed around a bucket which was stuffed with more than $170. In my excitement, I would leave the bucket at the venue, with all the money in it. Luckily it was still there the next week, and the money was distributed to the performers when I ran into them next. At an open mic, at Comedy Works, even at a crazy El Chorito comedian-wedding after party.

Holiday Ha Ha Ha 2018 took place on a Tuesday night. The Sunday prior I had flown back from my Los Angeles comedy visit. I wrote ten entrepreneur jokes on the plane. I told them all at the Irish Rover Open Mic on Monday night. I told the half that did better, later that night at Lion's Lair. On Tuesday I told the three best ones during my set.

Being able to turn over material for a real gig was a tremendous accomplishment for someone who half a year earlier could only get on stage and blackout. For someone whose jokes were four times too long and not nearly funny enough to pass muster.

I had come a long way, and in many ways, I felt like I had arrived. Here were some cool kids from the local comedy scene at my show, talking to me, having fun because of something that would not have happened, without my hard work.

Did I rest on my laurels and go out to celebrate? If you have the bug for stand-up comedy you can probably guess what I did next. Unable to let the honeymoon feeling last, I immediately sought out more mic time. There was new material to work on!

After packing up my car in several trips, I went to two more open mics that night, both within walking distance of the show. The first was a nearly empty Scruffy Murphy's, and after that Black Buzzard, a rock and roll stage beneath an Oskar Blues Brewery restaurant.

At Black Buzzard, hosted by Janae Burris, I got on stage pumped up by the confidence of my earlier show. I did fine. Nothing incredible. The crowd was small and tired. It was after midnight. But something interesting did happen.

I followed a very funny comedian who also struggled to get laughs. He looked very familiar. After I got off stage I talked to him and asked him how I might know him. I even thought his material sounded familiar, but I was sure he wasn't local.

The day before I had started a documentary series on Amazon Prime called Inside Jokes. It was like Hoop Dreams but for comedians trying to get into the Just For Laughs comedy festival. It centered on a group of comedians from New York City and Los Angeles.

The first episode focuses on the Los Angeles comedians, including Simon Gibson. It was the only episode I had watched so far.

This man at the bar that I had followed on stage was Simon Gibson.

I had several reactions.

One was a thrill that I was in the company of a TV star. Was this the future that I could have if I kept at this dream?

The other reaction was, why is this TV star getting on stage after midnight on a weeknight and doing jokes for an unreceptive crowd in a city far from home? (Spoiler alert) After he told me that in the last episode of Inside Jokes he performs at Just For Laughs, I was even more confused.

I guess it makes sense. I had just had the biggest accomplishment of my young comedy career. And here I was grinding out more stage time.

Even after the huge success he had enjoyed, because of the love of the game, and the desire to keep grinding and getting better, this was exactly where he should be.

As I fell asleep that night, jacked up with the adrenaline of a successful show, I smiled at something that had happened as I left the venue with my last armload of supplies.

There were still about a dozen audience members chatting amongst themselves. One of them grabbed me as I attempted a hasty escape. He said, "I had a rough day at work today, and needed that, thanks for all the laughs."

I was so touched by the comment that when I had time to reflect on it, it brought tears to my eyes.

I also laughed at the absurdity of it all. The idea that me, who had never been behind a comedy microphone just six months earlier, could create a positive experience for comedians and audience members, was crazy.

But it did happen, and I wouldn't trade the experience for anything.

The Big Show: Holiday Ha Ha Ha

Not Good Yet, The Closer

Comedy is a lot like Slumdog Millionaire. The movie hinges on the unbelievable idea that a man on a trivia show could know every answer to the questions he is asked because during his life he experienced the answer to every question.

A comedy set is just like that. I can look at one of my setlists, and see jokes about Airbnb, sports, and Denver. Well, I'm an Airbnb host that has played sports and lives in Denver. The best comedy is personal and the life experiences I have had make up my comedy.

One of the advantages I have over younger comedians is that I have lived a large portion of my life already. I have been around the world, I have done dumb things in college, and smart things in an office, and silly things at concerts, and have had so many wonderful and terrible experiences to draw upon for my jokes.

As I have exercised my comedy-writing muscle it has become easier for me to generate content. I will read something in a book, or hear something on TV that will remind me of a memory from twenty years ago that I think I can turn into a joke, and I will jot it down in Evernote on my phone. Later I will go through all those ideas and write longer-form material.

When I started I couldn't even generate enough ideas to write a few new jokes a day. Now I generate a dozen ideas a day. More than I can use. I now write with more purpose and a better understanding of the craft of comedy. I look for opportunities to harness the comedic power of contrast. Six months ago I thought contrast was only a TV setting.

When I get stage time, which is often more than five times per week, I am more purposeful. I have written goals. Do an act out. Make eye contact with an audience member. Talk more slowly. Talk more quickly. Leave the mic in the stand. And more.

Completing this book means I have accomplished one of my comedy goals. It is time for new ones.

In 2019 I want to be accepted into a comedy festival, be asked to join someone else's show, put on more comedy shows around Denver, write better jokes, perform in five new states, record a short comedy album and find a way to distribute it, and sell one hundred copies of this book.

It is important to me to have goals, so when I accomplish them I can celebrate them. Comedy is a never-ending treadmill, if you don't celebrate some successes you'll never enjoy yourself.

Although many things have changed for me and comedy, one thing has not. Every time I reach some new peak in my comedic journey, it is only a few hours, or days, before I am knocked back down several pegs. I bomb with new material at an open mic. I watch a week-old video and think of ways I am already better than that. I will see another comedian do something amazing, and wonder when I will have that skill. All of these things point to one central theme:

That I am not good yet. But with each setback and accomplishment, I am getting less not good, at a faster and faster pace. Who knows what the future will hold. I hope it sees me in your town or city getting strangers to laugh because I have learned there is almost nothing as exhilarating, as enjoyable, and as redemptive as that.

I hope to see you out there, please drop me a note and let me know how you would improve this book or what you enjoyed. Let me know how I can say hi when I get to your neck of the woods. Use the web form at www.markmasters.co.

If you are thinking about doing stand-up comedy, I have two things to say. Be prepared to work at it, and DO IT, already. You won't be good, but I believe in you anyways. Get out there and have fun!

I end many of my comedy sets with the words "let's see each other again". It doesn't really apply in this context of author and reader, but if I were to say it, maybe it would mean that I might have a future book in me, with updates on my 2019 goals and the adventures of a mediocre comic. Instead of the not good one you just finished reading about.

Not Good Yet, The Closer

So, my friends, it's that time I guess.

Let's see each other again.

Thank You, Stay Connected

Thank you for reading my book. Please leave a review for it online and tell a friend about it. It makes a big difference and just takes a moment.

www.notgoodyet.com

I really do hope readers reach out and stay in touch. Drop me a note. There is a web form at www.markmasters.co.

Appendix: Photos

Special thanks to my parents for the 1977 photo that appears on the back cover. The front cover photo was taken October 2018 in New York City.

Here are some more photos that complement the stories in this book.

Before My First Ever Open Mic at The Irish Rover

A typical Denver Open Mic Sign Up List

Appendix: Photos

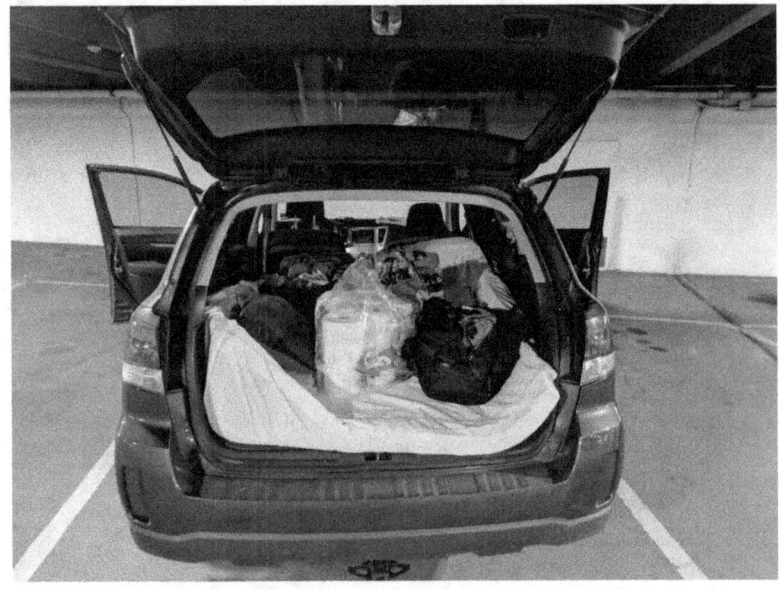

The morning after the car camp story

3 Kings Tavern Open Mic (yes, that's a cat)

Appendix: Photos

Locked out of an open mic, making do outside

Lion's Lair Open Mic

Appendix: Photos

Black Buzzard Open Mic (yes, that's a Mog)

Rolling into the first show I organized

Appendix: Photos

Set up for the first show I organized

Backstage at Comedy Works New Talent Night

Appendix: Photos

On stage at Comedy Works New Talent Night

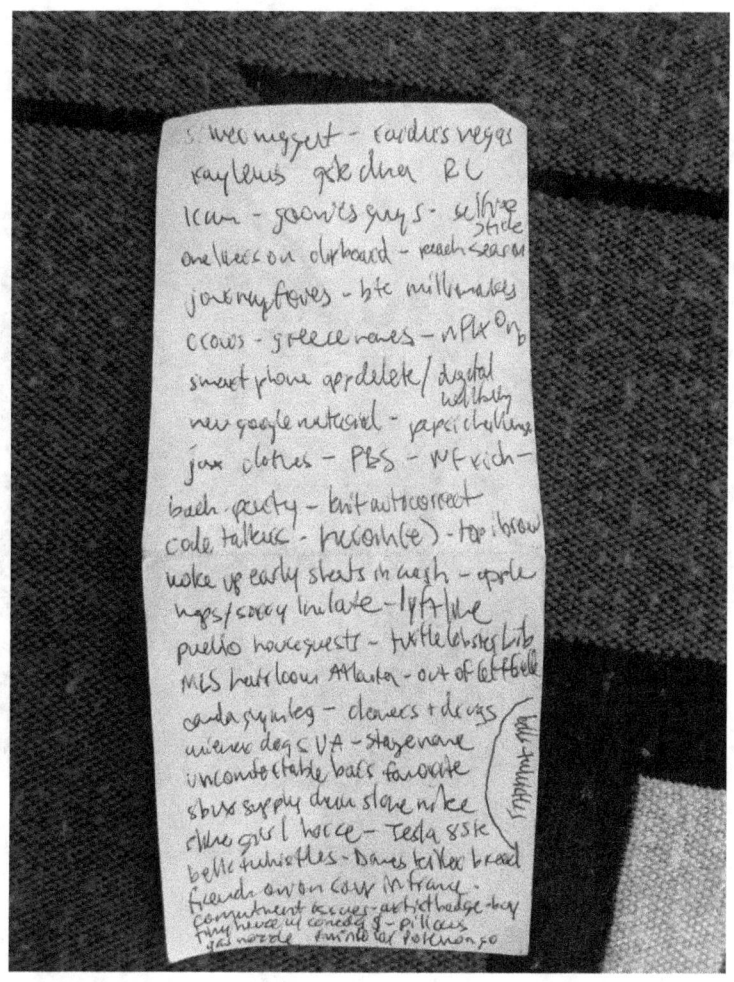

About 5 months in, every bit I have

The Santa Fe performance (yes, that's the wrong mic to use)

My trusty notebook, one of several I filled, and a free beer

Holiday Ha Ha Ha, show I organized and hosted

After the Holiday Ha Ha Ha Show with all the performers

Appendix: Photos

With Simon Gibson after Black Buzzard Open Mic

*Visiting New York City with big dreams, but still ...
Not Good Yet*

www.ingramcontent.com/pod-product-compliance
Lightning Source LLC
Chambersburg PA
CBHW070423010526
44118CB00014B/1876